PEARLS SELLS OUT

Other *Pearls Before Swine* Collections

The Saturday Evening Pearls

Macho Macho Animals

The Sopratos

Da Brudderhood of Zeeba Zeeba Eata

The Ratvolution Will Not Be Televised

Nighthogs

This Little Piggy Stayed Home

BLTs Taste So Darn Good

Treasuries

The Crass Menagerie

Lions and Tigers and Crocs, Oh My!

Sgt. Piggy's Lonely Hearts Club Comic

Gift Book

Da Crockydile Book o' Frendsheep

PEARLS SELLS OUT

A *Pearls Before Swine* Treasury

by Stephan Pastis

Andrews McMeel
Publishing,LLC

Kansas City • Sydney • London

Pearls Before Swine is distributed internationally by United Feature Syndicate.

Pearls Sells Out copyright © 2009 by Stephan Pastis. All rights reserved. Printed in the United States of America. No part of this book may be used or reproduced in any manner whatsoever without written permission except in the case of reprints in the context of reviews. For information, write Andrews McMeel Publishing, LLC, an Andrews McMeel Universal company, 1130 Walnut Street, Kansas City, Missouri 64106.

09 10 11 12 13 BAM 10 9 8 7 6 5 4 3 2 1

ISBN-13: 978-0-7407-7396-9
ISBN-10: 0-7407-7396-8

Library of Congress Control Number: 2009921629

www.andrewsmcmeel.com

Pearls Before Swine can be viewed on the Internet at
www.comics.com/pearls_before_swine

These strips appeared in newspapers from August 7, 2006, to February 16, 2008.

A special thanks to the *Pasadena Star-News* for their permission
to reprint the excerpt on page 8.

The plush animals on the cover were provided courtesy of Aurora (www.auroragift.com).

For Staci, who does all the responsible adult things
so that I can be a kid. I love you.

Introduction

Some cartoonists have wonderful stories about getting their first cartoon published when they were just a kid. Take Charles "Sparky" Schulz for example. As a child, long before he created *Peanuts*, Sparky drew a great picture of his dog Spike that was published in the nationally syndicated feature *Ripley's Believe It or Not.*

The story of my first published cartoon is not as wonderful.

The story of my first published cartoon is one of incompetence and fraud.

You see, the local paper in my community was called the *Pasadena Star-News*. And one page of the Sunday comics section was devoted to the drawings of young local kids. It was called "P. Wellington Woof's Kids' Korner," and if they printed your cartoon, you got the thrill of seeing it in print plus a check for two dollars.

As a baseball fan, I decided to draw a member of my hometown team, the Los Angeles Dodgers, sliding into second base. For reasons unknown, the judges picked my drawing for publication and printed it at the top of the page.

The first thing to note about my drawing (see page 8) is that it is by far the worst drawing for someone my age on the page. While kids younger than me were drawing cool race cars, robots, and roller skaters, I had this strange big-nosed man vibrating his way into second base.

But that's not the incompetent part.

The incompetent part is that after drawing this wonderful picture titled "Go Dodgers" and going to all the trouble of drawing two Dodgers logos and a "Go Dodgers" sign in the background, I then wrote "Angels" on the player's uniform.

This is no small error in a drawing titled "Go Dodgers."

But incompetence alone was not enough for young me and my publishing debut. So I decided to throw in a little fraud.

You see, if you look carefully at the caption under my cartoon, you'll see they've included the age I gave them: "Stephan Pastis, 11."

But I wasn't eleven.

P. Wellington Woof's Kids' Korner

Conducted Exclusively for JUNIOR ARTISTS AND WRITERS

Every week there are cash winners in the Star-News big P. Wellington Woof Contest. Send in your entry.

Stephan Pastis, 11, of San Marino, drew this picture entitled "Go Dodgers." He is a $2 winner.

Jamil Hai, 8, of Alhambra is a $2 winner for "The Clown and the Dog."

"Roller Skating is Back," according to Christina Reed, 11, of Altadena. She will receive a $2 check for giving us the scoop.

Kathy Horst, 12, of Arcadia tells us that this diligent athlete is "Trying Hard." Kathy will receive a $2 check for her drawing.

$2 goes to Gil Herrera, 13, of Temple City for his action-packed drawing "A Narrow Escape."

Kevin O'Dell, 10, of Arcadia is a $2 prize winner for his entry, entitled "Sleek."

$2 goes to Ray Warner, 12, of Pasadena for this original drawing, "My Dragster."

Matt N. Kroll, 11, of Sacramento envisions the "Future House Maid" to look like this. For his prophecy, Matt will receive a $2 check.

Wellington Club Rules Listed Here

1. DRAWINGS MUST BE DONE IN BLACK CRAYON OR SHARP HEAVY BLACK PENCIL OR PEN on 8" x 10" white paper. No colors, no lined paper. No other entries can be considered.

2. THE NAME, AGE AND ADDRESS must be written clearly on the back of each entry. Always include your city and zip code. If you are 15 or under you are eligible. No entries will be returned, all become the property of the department.

3. NEVER copy or trace anything. Someone is sure to recognize copied work and report it. If this happens we can no longer accept your entries.

4. ALL ENTRIES must be accompanied with a note from a parent or teacher saying that the drawing is the original work of the entrant. It should be written on the back of the entry.

5. ENTRIES should be sent to P. Wellington Woof, 525 E. Colorado Blvd., Pasadena 91109.

6. WINNERS will receive their awards by mail. Two weeks should be allowed for delivery.

7. Children of employes of the Star-News are not eligible to enter.

I was twelve. I had been twelve for more than eight months before the drawing was published. I'd like to say it was an accident on my part, but it wasn't. I lied.

I'm not sure why I lied. But I strongly suspect I did it to score a few more points with the judges. After all, an eleven-year-old is not expected to be quite as good an artist as a twelve-year-old.

Most important, the ruse worked. The drawing got published and I got my check, which—as you can see below—I inexplicably never cashed.

I'd like to say it was a twinge of guilt that kept me from cashing it. But I'm sure it wasn't. More likely, I was arrogant enough to think that one day I'd be a famous syndicated cartoonist and could publish the check in the introduction to one of my treasury books.

So if you're scoring this whole little early career venture at home, I'd say it came out:

Stephan: 1.

P. Wellington Woof: 0.

Oh sure, I suppose it could be argued that my admission of this fraud twenty-nine years after the fact could jeopardize my winnings. After all, the check still has not been cashed. But as an ex-lawyer, I would argue that nothing in the P. Wellington

Woof Rules printed at the bottom of the page expressly prohibited a twelve-year-old from saying he was eleven. The only age rule was that you had to be fifteen or under. Which I was. So there.

I guess all I can ask of you is that if you enjoy *Pearls*, please don't hold the inauspicious beginnings of my career against me. I was young. Mistakes were made.

Just set the whole ugly episode aside, enjoy the book, and relax.

Which is more than I can do.

I've got a check to cash.

Stephan Pastis

August 2009

Rat's line in the first panel ("throw ourselves upon the gears") is adapted from the words of a famous 1960s activist, Mario Savio, who once stood upon the roof of a police car and delivered this speech to a huge crowd of Berkeley students.

I think this is one of the few times the crocs have ever succeeded in eating a person.

In my adolescent years, my two cousins and I used to drive around in a Camaro doing things my mother would not have approved of. Thus, the reference to "three teens in a Camaro."

There was a little bit of discussion from one of my syndicate's salesmen about the wisdom of reworking the words of a prayer and the negative reaction that might provoke. Fortunately, there were few complaints.

When Bil Keane (creator of *Family Circus*) was writing the intro to *Macho Macho Animals*, he asked if there would be any strips in the book making fun of his strip. He wanted to know so he could include a discussion of those particular strips in the intro. I said yes. He asked me to describe them to him. That put me in the somewhat awkward position of saying to Bil Keane about his beloved characters: "Okay, well let's see, Dolly and Jeffy are alcoholics in a bar, and oh yeah, Jeffy is wearing a wife-beater undershirt."

| DID YOU HEAR ABOUT THE NEW RULE REQUIRING ALL COMIC STRIPS TO AGE THEIR CHARACTERS REALISTICALLY? EVEN THE OLD STRIPS LIKE 'FAMILY CIRCUS' HAVE TO DO IT. | THAT'S NUTS. THOSE 'FAMILY CIRCUS' KIDS WOULD HAVE TO BE ABOUT 50 YEARS OLD NOW. | YEAH... I GUESS HAVING THEM GROWN UP PROBABLY CHANGES THE STRIP A LITTLE. |

8/14

"Faster, Mommy, faster!"

This pose of the kids came straight out of a *Family Circus* book I own, only the kids weren't fat, smoking, and in their forties.

| THIS NEW RULE ABOUT COMIC STRIPS HAVING TO AGE THEIR CHARACTERS REALISTICALLY HAS REALLY CHANGED "FAMILY CIRCUS." | HOW SO? | WELL, WHEN THE KIDS ARE IN THEIR FIFTIES, IT'S... ...I DUNNO... *DIFFERENT.* | DIFFERENT HOW? |

8/15

"Get a job, Billy."

| I GUESS THE CREATORS OF 'FAMILY CIRCUS' DECIDED IT WAS JUST TOO RIDICULOUS TO HAVE 50-YEAR-OLD "KIDS" PLAYING WITH TOYS. | SO WHAT ARE THEY DOING NOW? | THEY'RE GIVING ALL THE NOW GROWN-UP KIDS MORE ADULT-ORIENTED LIVES...BUT I DON'T KNOW...I THINK IT LOSES SOME OF ITS CHARM. |

8/16

"And remember...No telling Mommy I shot my probation officer."

I like to make fun of Jeffy the most, because I know the grown-up Jeff Keane personally and enjoy ridiculing him.

Unlike with *Family Circus*, I do not know and have never met the creators of *Blondie*, so I have no idea what they think of strips such as this.

I like the drawing on both this and the next strip. It doesn't totally suck.

If I'm not mistaken, I think Darby Conley (creator of *Get Fuzzy*) wrote this punch line. I read him the strip over the phone and told him I couldn't think of anything to say in the last panel. He gave me "Cockiest. Cows. Ever."

When I was at the University of California at Berkeley, I went to some classes that must have had more than four hundred students in them. I almost always sat in the far back of the auditorium so I could read the newspaper. I remember that I stayed late one day to ask the professor a question, and when I got up to him, all I could think to myself was, "So *this* is what the professor looks like."

When I was at UCLA law school, I absolutely dreaded the possibility of being called on in class. Those other students were about the smartest group of people I'd ever been around, and compared to them I felt like a big fat idiot.

The original first panel of this did not say "Smittys." It had the last name of someone I knew in high school. But after I did it, I realized I hadn't seen the guy in years and didn't know how he'd feel about it, so I nixed his name and made one up instead.

This is sort of a misguided strip in that it's inconsistent with the Guard Duck's cool persona. Sure, he's violent, but he doesn't freak out or panic like this. More evidence that I often have no idea what I'm doing.

A rare six-panel strip. Sometimes the pauses seem essential to me (panels three and five) and so I include them. Other cartoonists, like Scott Adams, almost never vary from their daily three-panel format. I'm not sure which approach is right.

When I found out that Tom Richmond, the great artist for *MAD Magazine*, was coming to Santa Rosa to speak at the Charles M. Schulz Museum, I asked him if he would come over to my house and help me do this cartoon. He very kindly agreed. He downloaded like three or four images of Barbra Streisand from the Internet, sat down, and whipped out this caricature in about ten minutes. It was unbelievable. I would have spent ten hours trying to do it, and it would have come out a lot more like Rat's drawing than Tom's. He reciprocated a few months later by including a caricature of me in a TV parody he did for *MAD*. He made me a homeless guy diving in dumpsters for food.

This was one of the most popular strips of the year.

I think I cut and pasted that hamper from another strip I had done earlier. There was no way I was going to draw that thing twice. But each time the hamper appeared, a few sharp readers wrote in to ask, "Who in Rat and Pig's house wears socks?"

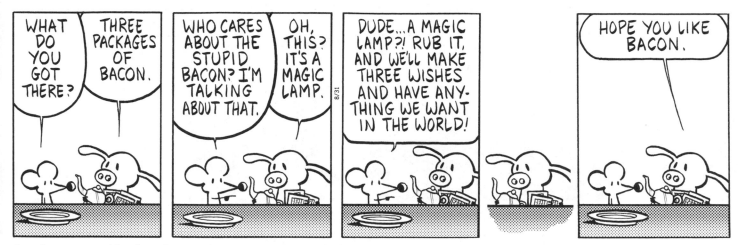

Another pause (the fourth panel). Sometimes I include them and sometimes I don't. It all depends on the particular joke.

This strip was drawn years before it appeared. I kept putting it off because I feared reader reaction to the idea of Rat speaking to God.

Zebra's line in the last panel is off-kilter, and it bothers me every time I read it. It's unnecessarily long and distracts from the joke. Those post–punch line comments almost always need to be shorter. A few words at most.

For some reason, Danny Donkey seems to resonate with people. If a few months go by with no Danny Donkey, I get a lot of e-mail asking for him.

The San Francisco Zoo has a great exhibit of these little guys, which is where I got the idea for this strip. One of them really does keep watch like that. They do not, however, manufacture illegal liquor. I need to say that so I don't get sued by any meerkats.

I appear to have cut and pasted the art from panel one and placed it in panel two. That's downright lazy and unbecoming of a syndicated cartoonist.

This was a very popular croc strip. I think if we ever animate individual *Pearls* strips, this would be a good one to use.

I think that's supposed to be me standing there. Given that I drew this, you'd think I'd know that sort of thing.

If you've never heard a Piccolo Pete, let me just tell you, it's very loud when someone lights three of them on your front porch in the middle of the night. Someone I know pretty well might have done that to some friends of his.

I think I wrote this while A-Rod was in a big slump. I think he came out of the slump right before this strip ran, making the strip seem dated. Ahh, the ever-present risk of trying to work current events into your strip.

This was another popular croc strip. I drew it the same day I drew the August 11, 2006, prayer strip, but separated their publication by a month so that they would not appear repetitive.

I gave the original of this strip to the owner of the café where I write *Pearls*. He hung it on the wall of the café. I figured I owed him since I buy one cup of coffee and proceed to sit there for three hours every day. I am not your ideal customer.

I thought making Larry's son a vegetarian was a decent wrinkle to add to Larry's already difficult life. I'm often asked if I'm a vegetarian. I am not, although I don't eat a whole lot of meat.

Larry's line here is one of my favorite croc lines, and I almost made it the title of one of the *Pearls* box calendars. It would have been called, *Me No Read But Look How Smart Me Is.*

When in doubt, give a character big, blown-up eyes and puffy lips.

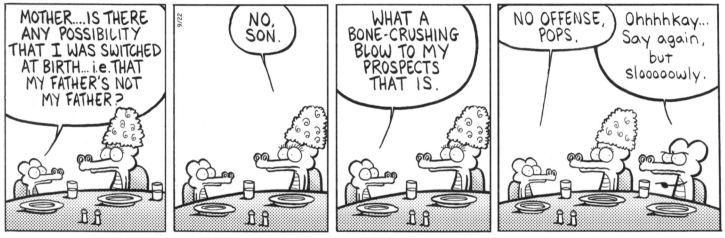

This strip is a bit out of whack. The Larry-Junior relationship should be as depicted in the September 20, 2006, strip. Junior is smarter than his dad, but he loves him and they're close. Here, Junior is just contemptuous of him. I make a lot of mistakes like this when I'm first learning who a character is and how he should interact with the others.

This fax machine is modeled after the fax machine in my house. If I'm ever superfamous and dead and they give tours of my house, I would expect a tour guide to point to that fax machine and say, "This was the actual fax machine used in the *Pearls* strip dated September 24, 2006."

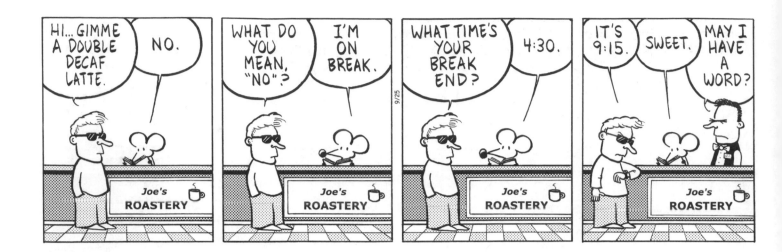

Most of the country did not see this strip. I'm still unclear as to exactly what happened, but apparently, at around the time this strip was supposed to run, there was a tragic story in the news about some children who died and it involved a washing machine. People at my syndicate who knew more than I did thought the strip would therefore be in bad taste, so most of the country saw a repeat that day.

This was a rare experiment for Danny Donkey. Up to this point, he existed only as a character in Rat's imagination. But during this week of strips, he came to life. I think that's the only time I've done that with him.

This six-strip Danny Donkey series was meant to run during the course of a Monday through Saturday. But my syndicate, worried again, decided it was too edgy, which I thought was a bit crazy. Too many references to beer, getting "loaded," etc. So the compromise was to split the series up. Two would run this week, and four would run the next. Also, we would bury this particular strip on a Saturday, where fewer people would see it.

In all my time with my syndicate, they've really been very good about letting me do my thing. But for whatever reason, they interfered more with the strip this particular month than at any time before or since. It was getting so that we were talking every few days. But this particular strip was sort of a breaking point.

Weeks before this was scheduled to run, the syndicate called me to ask if I could delete the beer references in the last panel. I said that I had always shown the characters drinking beer and didn't see anything wrong with it. They then suggested—rather unbelievably—that I change the beer to cookies. I couldn't believe it.

Angry and frustrated, I wrote a two-page e-mail to the syndicate explaining that we couldn't keep doing this. It was ridiculous. I wasn't gonna keep looking over my shoulder every time I drew a strip, wondering what the syndicate might say. Thankfully, they listened. Other than some editing of one more strip two weeks later (October 14, 2006), they really left me alone after this.

In fairness, I have to add that I've been very lucky to have my syndicate over the years. A lot of the other syndicates would not have let me do what I do. This was just a strange month, and I'm still not quite sure why it happened.

When I was a little kid, my dad owned a liquor store in Southern California. Using an old black-and-white photo I had of it, I drew the liquor store that appears in the third panel here. My reproduction of it was so accurate that after it appeared, I called my dad (who reads the strip every day in Phoenix) to ask what he thought of it. He said he didn't realize that it was his liquor store.

My idea with this series was to have Danny Donkey sort of be the anti-Hobbes (the tiger in *Calvin and Hobbes*): a stuffed animal who came to life but instead of being kind and wise was drunk and addicted to nicotine. It didn't really seem to catch on, though, so now I limit Danny Donkey to just being a character in Rat's children's books.

I always worry about how puns will be received, so sometimes I bury them on Saturday. To my surprise, this one turned out to be really popular.

I'm very harsh on real estate agents. I'm not sure why. Maybe it's because of how they call every small house "charming" and every run-down house a "great fixer-upper." Just once, I'd like them to show me a house and declare, "This one's a piece of crap."

It's fun to do a comic strip where you can just randomly discard gravity for the day. This could not happen in *Rex Morgan*.

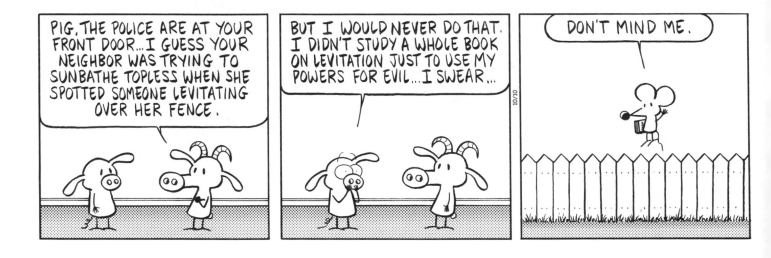

In my obsession with real estate agents, I've often noticed from their cheesy photos that many of the women like to wear showy scarves. Someone should explore this phenomenon.

Doonesbury's got nothing on me, baby. Look at that White House. Just look at it. I am so proud I could weep.

Okay, this is the last strip my syndicate changed for quite a while after my e-mail exchange with them. And what they changed was the last line. In the original last panel, Rat's line was "Just think of us as *Hi and Lois* on mescaline. Lots and lots of mescaline." The syndicate thought the drug reference would be too much for some newspapers. Thus, I changed it to the line you see here. Ironically, the current creator of *Hi and Lois*, Brian Walker, saw the strip and asked for the original. I had to explain that it contained the mescaline line, but he still wanted it, so I sent it. The original of this strip can be seen in the "Stuff You Ain't Never Seen Before" section of this book.

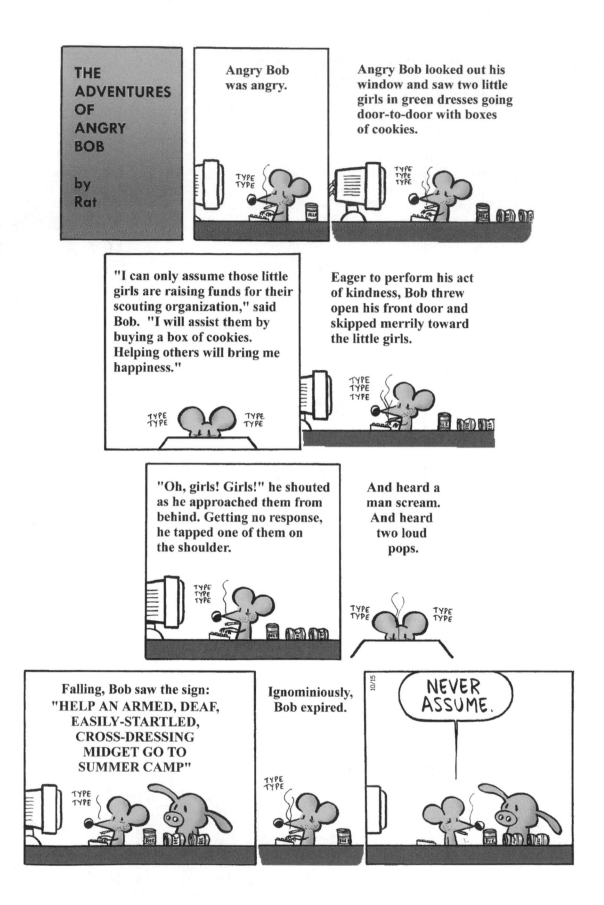

THE ADVENTURES OF ANGRY BOB

by Rat

Angry Bob was angry.

Angry Bob looked out his window and saw two little girls in green dresses going door-to-door with boxes of cookies.

"I can only assume those little girls are raising funds for their scouting organization," said Bob. "I will assist them by buying a box of cookies. Helping others will bring me happiness."

Eager to perform his act of kindness, Bob threw open his front door and skipped merrily toward the little girls.

"Oh, girls! Girls!" he shouted as he approached them from behind. Getting no response, he tapped one of them on the shoulder.

And heard a man scream. And heard two loud pops.

Falling, Bob saw the sign: "HELP AN ARMED, DEAF, EASILY-STARTLED, CROSS-DRESSING MIDGET GO TO SUMMER CAMP"

Ignominiously, Bob expired.

NEVER ASSUME.

Look at that authentically reproduced Scotch tape dispenser. It's almost like you could grab it right off the page. Well, it would be a little small. But you get the idea.

The *Miami Herald* did not run this strip, nor did they run the next one. They stated it was due to a production error. Some readers questioned that claim, given the fact that the strips concerned Fidel Castro and Cuba, an issue of great sensitivity in the Miami area.

An executive from Bob's Big Boy contacted me after he saw this strip. When I saw the e-mail address, I thought for sure I was being sued. As it turned out, he loved the strip.

Here I am tormenting poor real estate agents again. And look at that fine scarf.

This is the strip I used in the intro to the second *Pearls* treasury, *Lions and Tigers and Crocs, Oh My!* In the book, I noted that I didn't know whether people were going to find it funny or lame, as it hadn't run in papers yet. As it turned out, it wasn't a big hit. Now I wish I could go back and grab it out of the intro. Alas, it is too late. Oh, my difficult life.

This strip and the next one were big hits. I don't know what it is about song parodies, but people really seem to like them. For all of you Dylanites out there, I based this caricature on the photo of Dylan that appears on the *Blonde on Blonde* album cover.

Larry's a fun character to write for. He's dumb like Pig, but mean-spirited and rude.

Neville Chamberlain references are a good way to lose 95 percent of your audience for the day.

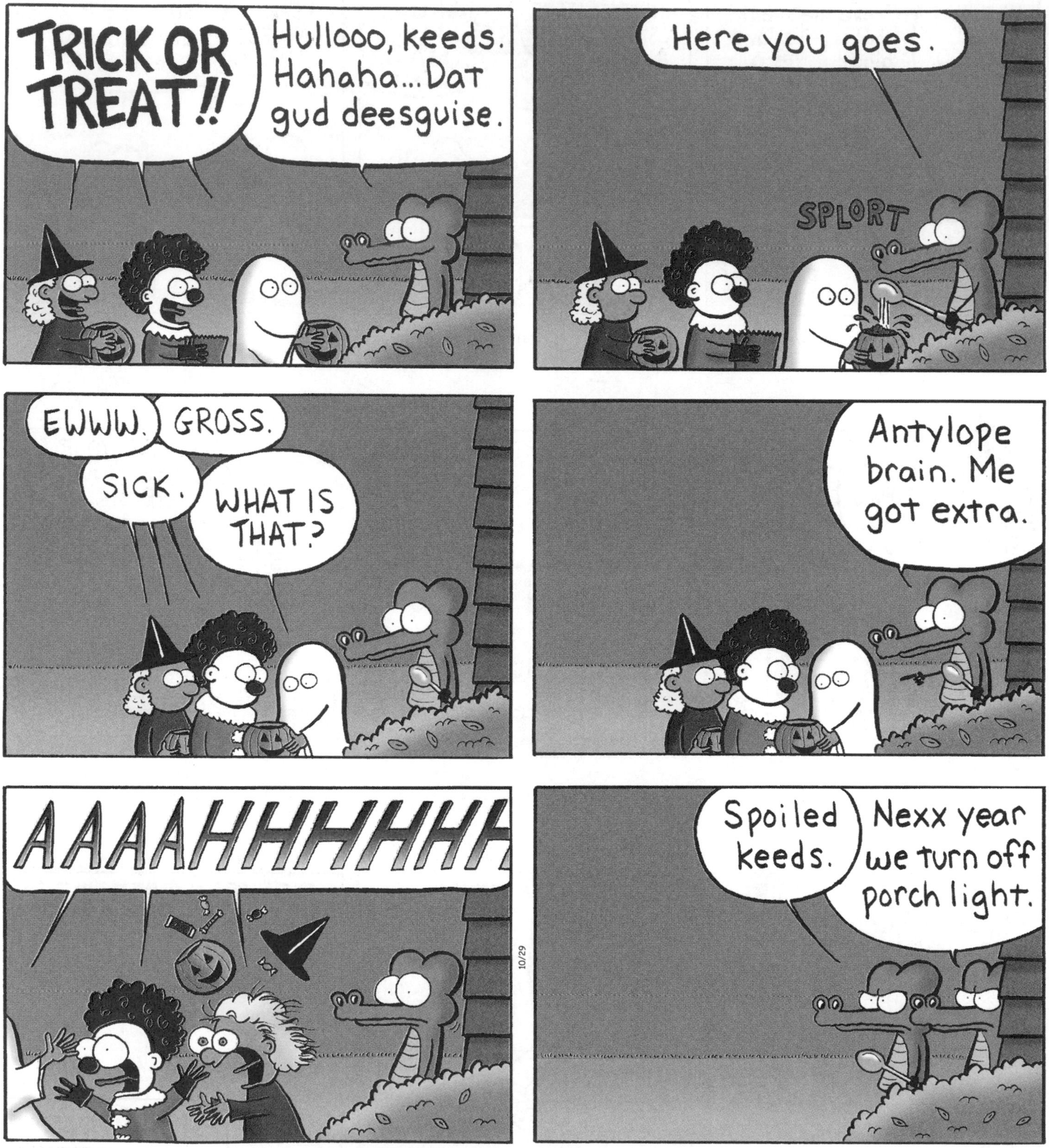
TRICK OR TREAT!!
Hullooo, keeds. Hahaha...Dat gud deesguise.
Here you goes.
SPLORT
EWWW.
GROSS.
SICK.
WHAT IS THAT?
Antylope brain. Me got extra.
AAAAHHHHHH
10/29
Spoiled keeds.
Nexx year we turn off porch light.

I just noticed something. The way Guard Duck is holding that weapon would make it very difficult for him to fire it. The trigger is about two feet in front of his wing. I need to spend more time fact-checking my work.

Oh, see now, I lied. Danny Donkey *did* make one more appearance outside the context of Rat's books. He came to life here for Halloween. If I wasn't so lazy, I would go back and change that earlier comment.

This was supposed to be my subtle little parody of Colin Powell at the United Nations presenting his "proof" of WMD in Iraq. The parody was so subtle that no one got it. That's what I call subtle.

See, I thought this comic would cause problems given that it mentions eating illegal aliens. But no, it drew no complaints. I swear to you, I have almost no idea which strips will cause problems and which won't.

You know, there's no way to say you like one of your own strips without looking like an arrogant fathead. That said, I like this strip.

It's fun to occasionally draw attention to the characters' nudity.

The "enemies list" is a reference to the enemies list once kept by Richard Nixon. It contained all sorts of people he disliked, from entertainers to athletes.

I am a big fan of the University of California's football team. This was my homage to the coach, Jeff Tedford, who has brought our football program from nothing to greatness. Unbelievably, during a press conference before the big USC-Cal football game, one of the reporters asked Tedford what he thought of this particular strip. His response was that he had never heard of *Pearls Before Swine*. I didn't care. *Pearls* had been mentioned at a Cal football news conference. My life was complete.

Declaring that the person you marry should have a tight rear end can cause problems on the comics page. Not unexpectedly, this drew a few complaints.

Months ago, 'Pearls' creator Stephan Pastis determined that one of his crocodile characters, Biff, was simply too dumb and delusional to live with the other crocodiles in the Zeeba Zeeba Eata Fraternity house. Thus, Stephan moved Biff into his own backyard, where he could care for him. We now rejoin the comic, already in progress.

I was planning on making Biff a regular character, but I ran out of ideas for him.

I'm sure this week of strips created a fair amount of confusion among newspaper readers. These are the days I'd like to be a fly on the wall when readers call their papers.

(Editor's Note: Due to a pagination error, the dialogue from today's Pearls Before Swine has been inadvertently omitted. From the limited portion that is viewable, it appears that the angry nun in panel (3) is scolding an inebriated monkey. For those of you who may be inconvenienced by the omission, we'd like to remind you that the angry nun/drunken monkey gag is about as hackneyed as one could imagine in contemporary comedy, and probably offered very little in the way of humor value. Thank you for your patience.)

I told Darby Conley (*Get Fuzzy*) that I wanted to do this, and he was nice enough to give me a bunch of *Get Fuzzy* panels to choose from.

Ironically, after these strips were created, I really did have an issue with one of the *Pearls* paginators (the people who lay out the comics page for newspapers). When I saw these strips coming up, all I could think was, "Oh man. He's gonna think these strips are about him." But the truth was that they weren't.

I was really hoping to open my front door the day after this strip appeared and see a case of Red Tail Ale waiting for me, courtesy of the good folks at Red Tail Ale. This did not occur.

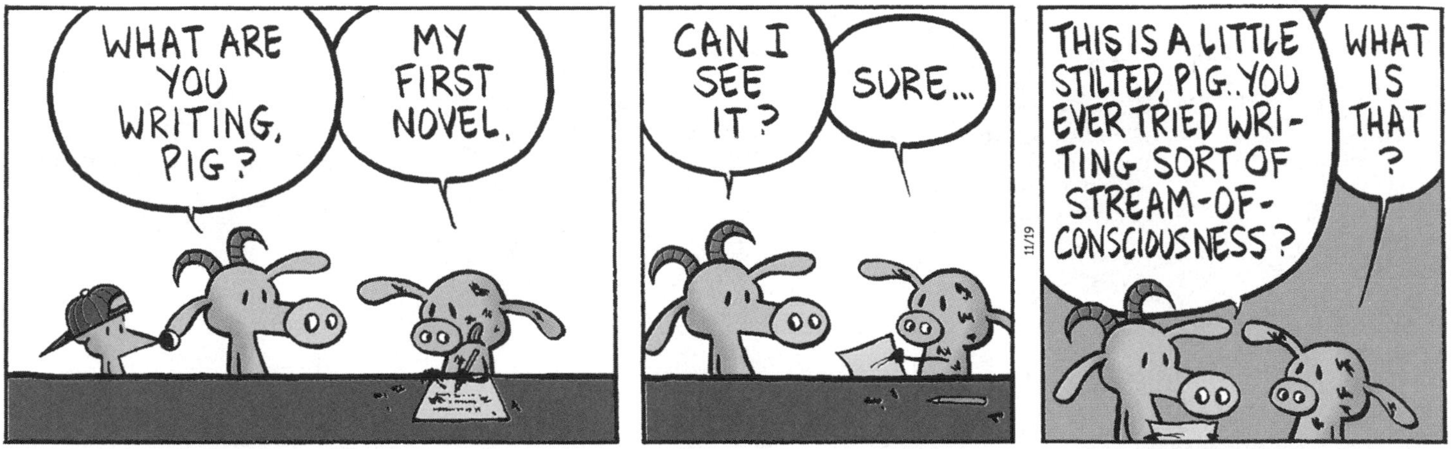
WHAT ARE YOU WRITING, PIG?
MY FIRST NOVEL.
CAN I SEE IT?
SURE...
11/19
THIS IS A LITTLE STILTED, PIG.. YOU EVER TRIED WRITING SORT OF STREAM-OF-CONSCIOUSNESS?
WHAT IS THAT?

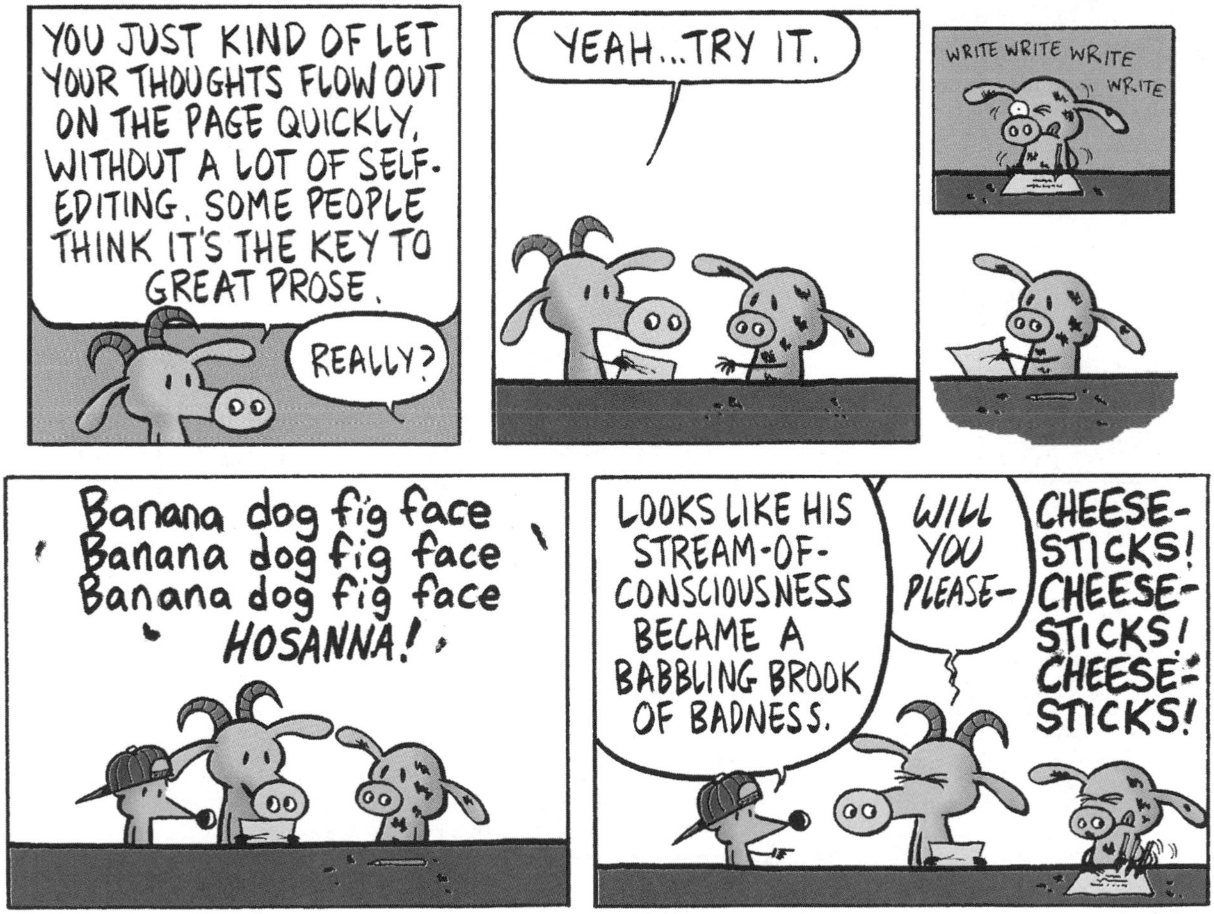
YOU JUST KIND OF LET YOUR THOUGHTS FLOW OUT ON THE PAGE QUICKLY, WITHOUT A LOT OF SELF-EDITING. SOME PEOPLE THINK IT'S THE KEY TO GREAT PROSE.
REALLY?
YEAH...TRY IT.
WRITE WRITE WRITE WRITE
Banana dog fig face
Banana dog fig face
Banana dog fig face
HOSANNA!
LOOKS LIKE HIS STREAM-OF-CONSCIOUSNESS BECAME A BABBLING BROOK OF BADNESS.
WILL YOU PLEASE-
CHEESE-STICKS! CHEESE-STICKS! CHEESE-STICKS!

I had to get one of my artistic friends, Justin Thompson, to show me how to draw an explosion crater. He drew it for me, and I copied his drawing here. I paid him zero dollars for his trouble. I figured my being a friend to him was payment enough.

The creator of *Pickles*, Brian Crane, asked if he could have the original of this. I sent it to him and he gave me a *Pickles* strip.

This was supposed to be a week-long series, but I got tired of it after only three strips and decided to stop the series. Because I didn't really like it, I buried it during Thanksgiving week, when I assumed less people were reading newspapers.

Middle-finger jokes are tricky, particularly on Sunday, when more kids are supposed to be reading the comics. That's why I put this on Thanksgiving weekend, again assuming that people were mostly out of town and not reading the funnies.

Man, I put myself in a lot of comic strips. Something's wrong with my sense of self.

I was lucky enough to visit the *Family Guy* studios in 2007. It was a lot of fun. I would love to have the freedom to write some of the jokes those guys write.

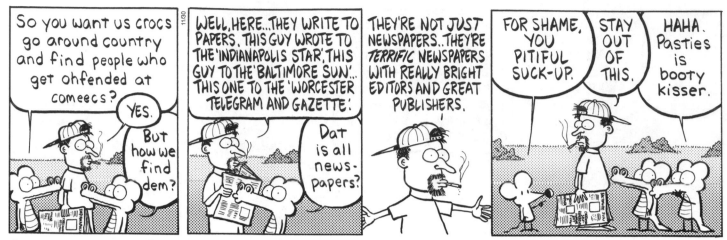

These newspapers really had printed complaints about *Pearls*. And I really was sucking up. I am not above that.

The current creator of *Snuffy Smith*, John Rose, contacted me after this strip appeared. He was amazingly gracious. I gave him the original of this strip and in exchange, he gave me an original *Snuffy Smith*. Giving out original strips is preferable to being sued.

Call me stupid, but I was amazed when this strip drew complaints. I just don't see "bite me" as remotely offensive.

I thought giving the Guard Duck a weakness could help add some depth to the character.

Story Update: 'Pearls Before Swine' cartoonist Stephan Pastis has sent his crocs on a mission to find and appease comic strip readers from coast to coast. We rejoin the story, already in progress.

Hullo, Meester and Mees Feegowitz. We hear you write letter to paper saying 'Pearls' is 'ohfensive.'

YEAH. WE DID. HOW COME?

Because me agree.

...Now 'Beetles Baileys'... DERE'S a funny comic!

DARN RIGHT, SON.

ETHEL!! MORE BEER!!

Hullooo, Meester Pasties....Leesten. Me, Bob and Jimmy decide to veesit newspapers.

I DIDN'T TELL YOU TO DO THAT.

Yes. Me know. But we want spread goodwill wid comeec editors. We go Sacreemento, Fressno, Mowdesto and...Oh... Leetle probbum in Bakerfeeld.

WHAT HAPPENED IN BAKERSFIELD ?!?

Jimmy eat an editor.

HE WHAT

He was FOOD editor.

Dat not make it okay, Jimmy.

Strips like this will almost always trigger feedback from people in the cities mentioned. In this particular case, I listed all the cities in California's Central Valley that run *Pearls*. I figured a few shout-outs now and then can't hurt.

OKAY, GUYS, I CANCELLED YOUR TRIP AROUND THE COUNTRY BECAUSE I CAN'T HAVE YOU OUT THERE SLAMMING 'PEARLS' AND EATING FOOD EDITORS.

SO FROM NOW ON, YOU STAY HOME WHERE YOU CAN'T CAUSE ANY MORE PROBLEMS FOR THE STRIP.

CRUNCH

OKAY, SEE, NOW THAT'S A PROBLEM.

Say you sorry, Bob.

This was a little more graphic than usual, but I thought it looked funny, so I kept it.

I really did draw this with my left hand. Man, was it hard.

This was a very popular strip.

This was an old strip I really didn't like. It was actually part of a two-strip series. I delayed running it for about three years after it was drawn, which is why it looks so different. I killed the second one completely. The second strip can be in the "Stuff You Ain't Never Seen Before" section at the back of the book.

I'm not quite sure why I went to all that trouble drawing Goat walking into the house in the seventh panel. Clearly, I was feeling very ambitious that day.

I want to say for the record that I always pull over for the guy behind me, as long as there's a place to pull over. I don't understand why some drivers refuse to do that, even when it's obvious the driver behind them is in a hurry. This is yet another reason to hate stupid people and their stupid people ways.

When I wrote this strip, it made a lot of sense to me. Then it appeared in newspapers and it no longer made sense to me. Did Pig's grandmother die? Was Pig referring to her tombstone? Did her face just begin to look like stone? I have no idea. And I'm the creator.

Having a syndicated comic strip is a great platform for ripping on expressions you hate.

The phrase "I just turn on my monkey and it makes me feel good" sounds very dirty, but I can't explain why. It's great to try to use expressions like that on the comics page. People want to complain but can't, because they can't figure out quite what they should be complaining about.

This raises a lot of questions, like why can't the croc just reach over and eat Zebra also? My weak explanation is that Goat is standing in between them. I need to start thinking these things through.

I rarely try to do Christmas-themed strips, mostly because I'm drawing them in April or May, and it's hard to be thinking of Christmas in the spring. But for some reason I decided to make this an all-Christmas theme week.

I'm the only cartoonist whose Christmas-themed week uses the phrase "fatwa on the duck."

I like the fact that Larry's son, Junior, is not on the same page as his father. Adds extra tension to his father's life.

Look at that bendable straw in Pig's glass. Normally, the glasses I draw don't even have straws. That's the sort of artistic variation that keeps readers coming back.

I think I was probably influenced by *Calvin and Hobbes* here, in that it's a Sunday strip without a lot of words that relies more on pictures to carry the joke. I don't do these very often.

I'm not sure why it is that Pig sometimes wears clothes. It's sort of an oddity. Like everything else in this strip.

This baby thing was supposed to be a week-long series, but I drew one strip and lost interest. I have a very short attention span.

When I don't like a strip, I tend to hide it in the week after Christmas, on the assumption that fewer people are reading newspapers. That was the case with both this strip and the baby one on December 26, 2006.

This is the continuation of the gun series I first started running in August, 2005, and discussed in the last treasury book, *The Crass Menagerie*. I thought the series could create problems (certain editors really do not like strips dealing with gun violence), so I broke it up. I ran one strip in August, most of the series here in December, and the rest on random Saturdays the next year.

If I had any guts, I would have spelled "ass" with the swear symbols "@$$." But I don't. The Man has beaten me down.

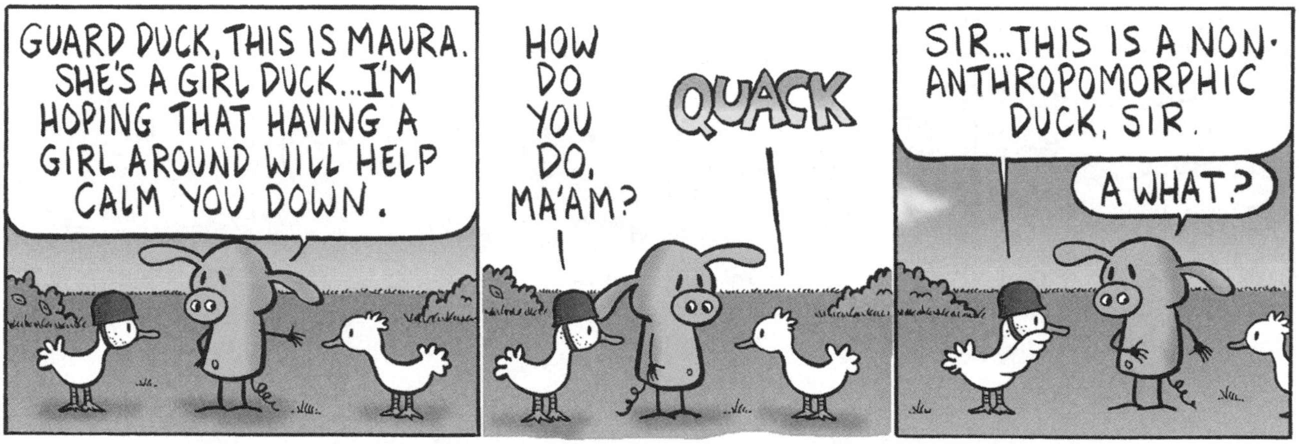
GUARD DUCK, THIS IS MAURA. SHE'S A GIRL DUCK...I'M HOPING THAT HAVING A GIRL AROUND WILL HELP CALM YOU DOWN.
HOW DO YOU DO, MA'AM?
QUACK
SIR...THIS IS A NON-ANTHROPOMORPHIC DUCK, SIR.
A WHAT?

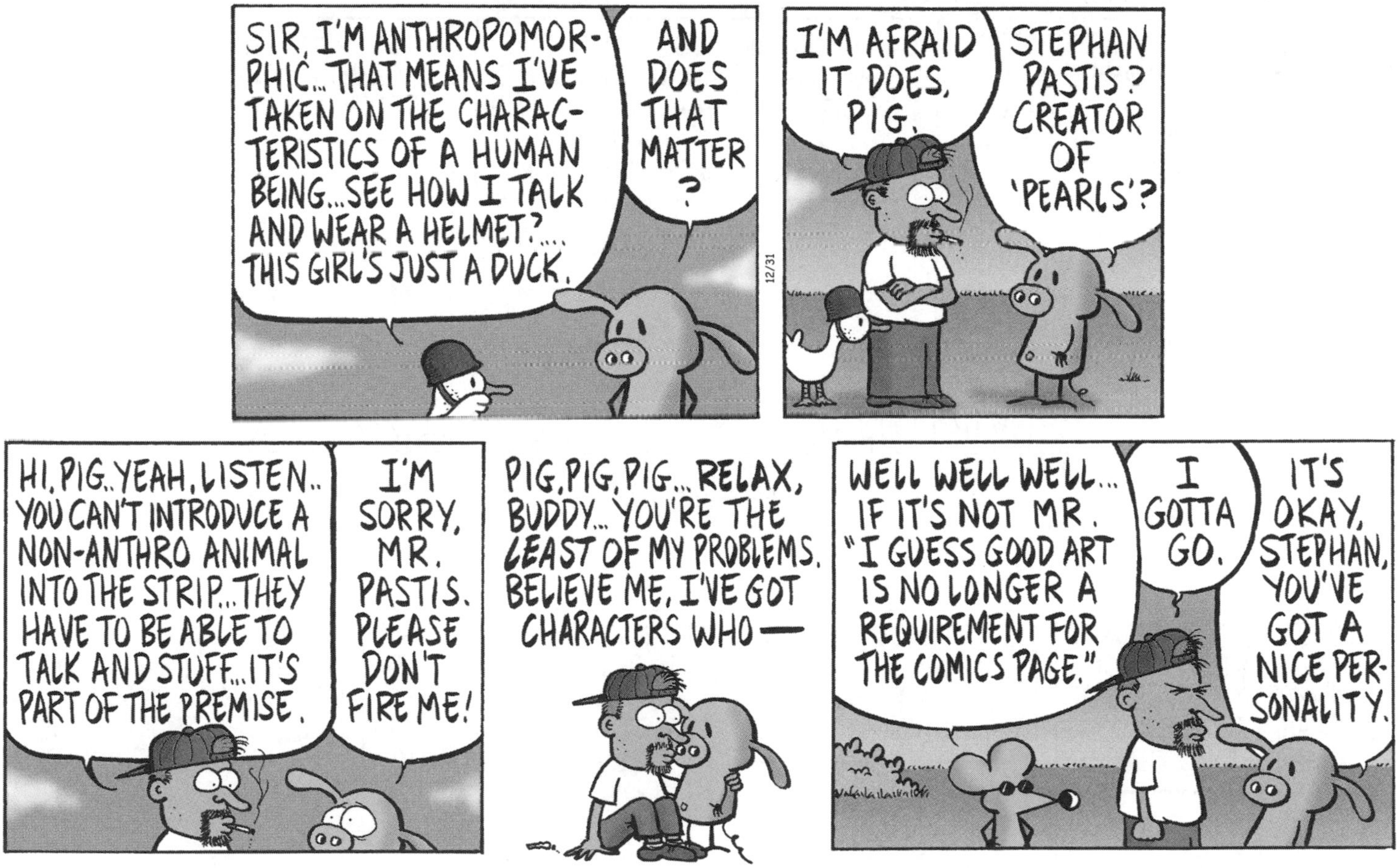
SIR, I'M ANTHROPOMORPHIC... THAT MEANS I'VE TAKEN ON THE CHARACTERISTICS OF A HUMAN BEING...SEE HOW I TALK AND WEAR A HELMET?.... THIS GIRL'S JUST A DUCK.
AND DOES THAT MATTER?
12/31
I'M AFRAID IT DOES, PIG.
STEPHAN PASTIS? CREATOR OF 'PEARLS'?
HI, PIG..YEAH, LISTEN.. YOU CAN'T INTRODUCE A NON-ANTHRO ANIMAL INTO THE STRIP...THEY HAVE TO BE ABLE TO TALK AND STUFF...IT'S PART OF THE PREMISE.
I'M SORRY, MR. PASTIS. PLEASE DON'T FIRE ME!
PIG, PIG, PIG... RELAX, BUDDY... YOU'RE THE LEAST OF MY PROBLEMS. BELIEVE ME, I'VE GOT CHARACTERS WHO—
WELL WELL WELL... IF IT'S NOT MR. "I GUESS GOOD ART IS NO LONGER A REQUIREMENT FOR THE COMICS PAGE."
I GOTTA GO.
IT'S OKAY, STEPHAN, YOU'VE GOT A NICE PERSONALITY.

The relationship between the Guard Duck and Maura turned out to be more popular than I anticipated.

Look at that little curlicue drawn by Rat in the air. I think I got that idea from the movie *Pulp Fiction*, where Uma Thurman draws a square in the air with her finger, and the square is visible on the screen.

I don't really know what chateaubriand is. It just sounded like something fancy you'd order in an expensive restaurant. I'm hoping it actually is a type of food.

This strip seemed to touch a lot of people.

This is another strip from the gun series that I started running in August, 2005.

I often have trouble with Zebra's arms when they extend out across his mane. The problem with it is that the arm is just a solid black line and it disappears in the solid black mane. Thus, I have to carve out a strange white outline around the arm, as I did in the last panel here. Man, I would be so good at cartooning if it didn't involve cartooning.

Oh boy. This strip created the single biggest controversy I've experienced in my six years of doing *Pearls*. The anger was over the use of the name "Ataturk." Mustafa Atatürk was a Turkish leader who, as I came to find out, is absolutely revered in his home country. The fact that I used the name for a llama who spits (combined with the fact that I'm Greek) created an incredible firestorm that I absolutely did not intend or anticipate. I knew virtually nothing about Atatürk and just liked the sound of the name. There were more than 2,500 complaints, mostly from people in Turkey. They were some of the most hate-filled messages I've ever received, and more than a few of them contained death threats. Some folks even created YouTube videos ridiculing me over it (just enter "Stephan Pastis" on YouTube to see them). The most amazing thing of all, though, was an actual letter from the Turkish ambassador to the United States demanding an apology. The whole experience was pretty unbelievable.

Another strip I held on to for a while, I think because of the reference to a "one night stand." What's controversial for the comics page would not be controversial in almost any other entertainment medium.

I think I cut and pasted some art here, judging from the remarkable similarities of the last two panels. A better cartoonist would avoid this sort of thing.

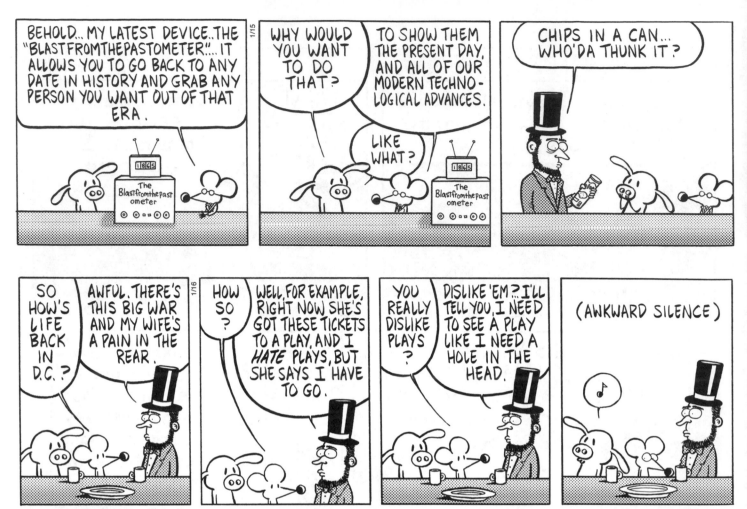

Okay, three things here.

Thing Number One: A couple months before this was scheduled to run, I saw the identical joke on the TV show *The Office*, which almost made me hold back on the strip because I thought everyone would accuse me of ripping off the show. But I loved the joke and I had written it myself, and so I wasn't going to pull the strip.

Thing Number Two: I was absolutely stunned by the complaints this particular week of strips generated. All of the complainers who wrote said it was in very poor taste to make fun of the Lincoln assassination. Apparently, 142 years is not enough time for people to come to terms with their grief over the Lincoln assassination. Of all the complaints I have ever received, I thought these were some of the most ridiculous.

Thing Number Three: One of the great ironies of this week of strips, at least to me, was that I had read a couple of terrific biographies on Lincoln and learned he had a great gallows sense of humor. He joked about death quite a lot. So from this I conclude that if Lincoln were alive today and saw these strips, he'd give me a big high five and probably take me out for a beer.

Man, I really liked this series. To heck with the oversensitive, weirdo complainers. They need to find themselves a hobby.

For all the readers upset over my perceived lack of respect for Lincoln, I'm sure this drawing of him getting hit in the face by a banana and swearing did not help.

I think Rat's line in the third panel was inspired by the Replacements' song, "Anywhere Is Better Than Here."

This was another strip that was supposed to be the beginning of a week-long series, but I got bored with the story line after only one strip and did not draw the others.

I think I did three or four different versions of this punch line, none of which was very good. Whenever that happens, it's probably a sign that something is wrong with the setup and the strip should probably be scrapped. It's just so hard to scrap a strip after you've already gone to the trouble of drawing it. One of the strips with the alternate punch lines appears in the back of the book in the section titled "Stuff You Ain't Never Seen Before."

My subtle little homage to my alma mater, the University of California at Berkeley, is on Junior's helmet.

This is the last of the gun series that I had begun running in August, 2005.

You know, I was wrong earlier. My syndicate did *not* stop trying to change the strip after the October 1, 2006, beer strip. They wanted to change this one also. The complaint from them here was about Rat's holding a rifle, which made absolutely no sense to me. Rat had talked about trying to buy a gun for a week and even said he wanted to shoot his neighbor. According to the syndicate, the difference with this particular strip was that I actually *showed* the rifle. The whole thing was just so crazy. I had grown up with countless Warner Bros. cartoons where Elmer Fudd actually shot Daffy Duck in the face and now, sixty years later, we couldn't show a rifle in a comic strip. Fortunately, after much discussion, they agreed to let me go with the strip as is.

I always liked the strips in *Calvin and Hobbes* where Calvin would pretend to be one of his many personas, like the detective "Tracer Bullet." So I tried to do my own version of that in this strip and the next, but it really came out bad. It just didn't fit the rhythm of my particular strip and looked like I was trying much too hard. Comic strips have to sort of spring from you spontaneously. When you work too hard at it or overthink things, it shows.

For this particular strip, I had to get the strainer out of the kitchen and set it on the drawing table in front of me. Man oh man, the things I won't do to bring you the artistic realism you've come to expect from *Pearls Before Swine.*

You know, I've got to say, this was one heck of a bad week of dailies. Almost all six of these strips are bad. If there was a way of giving refunds for just two pages of this otherwise fine book, I would do it.

For all that had happened to me during the Lincoln week, I fully expected an angry letter from some older person who had actually seen the Hindenburg explode right over their head. But alas, no complaints. Why you can make light of a 70-year-old tragedy but not a 142-year-old tragedy is beyond my powers of comprehension.

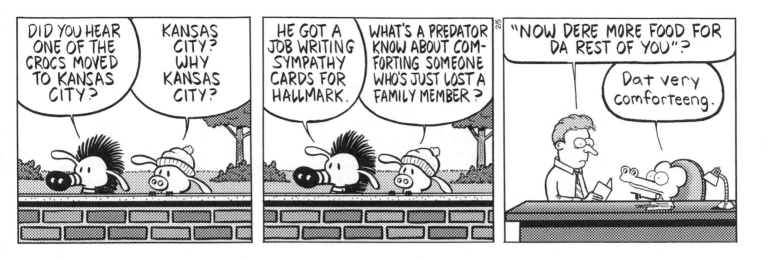

The second panel was a strange little "no-background" experiment. In retrospect, it looks a little odd in my strip.

If I remember right, I think I got a really complimentary e-mail from one of Hallmark's card designers after this strip came out. Perhaps it is a secret yearning of all Hallmark employees to use the phrase "you big fat pain in butt" in an anniversary card.

This strip is sort of a variation of another strip I did a few years earlier. (In the earlier strip, Pig says, "This burrito does not agree with me." Rat asks why. The burrito says, "Because he's a #$%#$#& moron and everything he says is wrong.") So I guess you could say I ripped myself off. I will be suing myself shortly.

In my opinion, the line after the punch line should never be longer than the punch line itself. That, of course, did not stop me from breaking that rule here. Why I did it, I don't know. The result is almost always a comic strip ending that is out of rhythm.

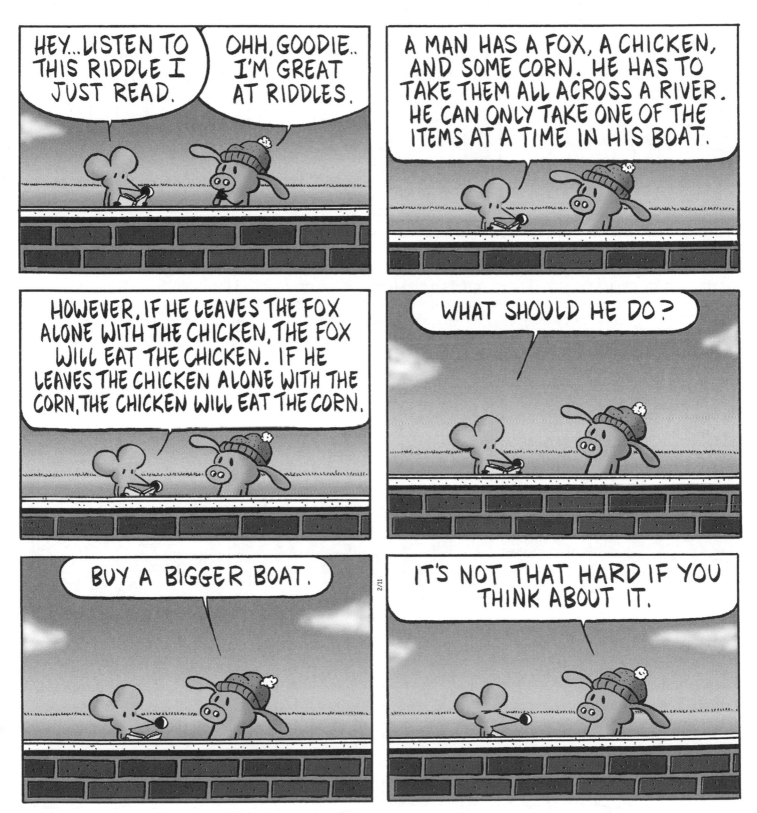

There really is an answer to Rat's riddle. I would type it all out, but it's very long and my fingers would get tired.

This was a very popular strip. Perhaps I had finally broken out of what I will call my month-long humor slump. You know, the funny thing is that I draw the strips many months in advance, and when they finally appear in newspapers, they do not appear in the order in which I drew them. When I'm determining which strips to run when, I just lay out all the strips I have stored up and have the luxury of picking the ones I want to run in any particular week (as opposed to most cartoonists, who are on very tight deadlines and have no choice but to run all the strips they drew that week). Thus, when a slump like this happens, it doesn't mean I sucked for a month of drawing. It just means that for one reason or another, when I was assembling the strips for publication, I assembled a sucky month's worth of strips.

Here's an example of a strip I thought was just okay but ended up getting a really positive reaction. It remains impossible for me to predict which ones will resonate with people.

I seem to be able to get away with pun strips if I add a panel at the end where I somehow indicate that I *know* it's a bad pun.

I think the Guard Duck has two poses: facing right and facing left. I don't think I've ever tried to draw him head-on. I wouldn't know how.

This, of course, triggered a few of the mandatory "How dare you make light of manic-depressive people" complaints. You are almost guaranteed to get complaints if you make light of any physical or mental disease/disorder.

In January, 2007, my good friend Bill Amend semiretired his excellent *FoxTrot* strip (he stopped doing the Monday through Saturday strips but continues publishing it on Sundays). I was fortunate enough to get a lot of the newspaper slots left by the departing *FoxTrot*. It's very rare for a cartoonist to actually retire these days, as most strips are handed off to someone else to draw. By retiring, a cartoonist does a tremendous favor to all the young cartoonists out there, in that he frees up newspaper space for their strips to be published. This was my tribute to him.

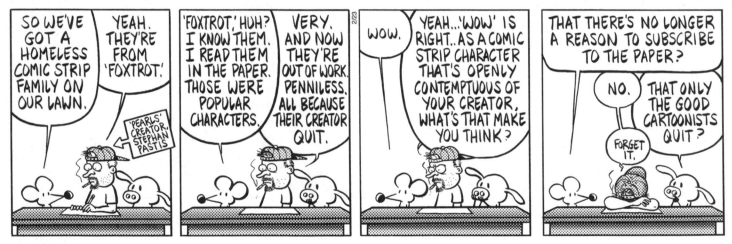

96

When I was done with this strip, I remember finding it a little confusing. It's sad when a cartoonist confuses himself with his own work.

Okay, here was a strip I thought would get a really positive reaction, and the reaction was just so-so. Same with the croc strip on February 28, 2007, below. And yet there are other croc strips that I cringe at, but people love. It's strange, but you learn after a while that individual strips have this crazy, unpredictable X factor. If it's there, it works, and if it's not, it doesn't.

I like meeting people for the first time and using information such as this for the conversation opener. I will say something like, "Hi. How are you? You ever wonder why the letters on your computer keyboard are not arranged alphabetically?" Typically, they smile, nod, and walk away, convinced that something is not quite right with me. I'd say that's a pretty accurate assessment.

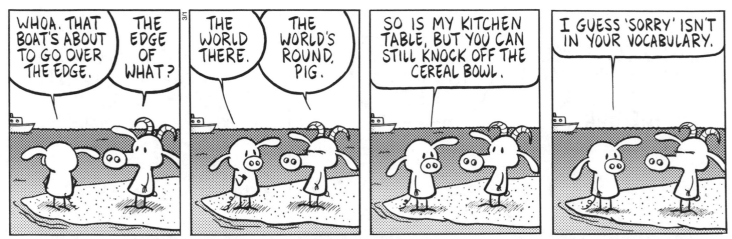

Rarely do strips come straight out of my life, but this one did. My eleven-year-old son, Thomas, and I were making sand castles at the beach and I told Thomas that a boat on the horizon was about to fall off the edge of the world. When he said the world was round, I said what Pig says there in the third panel. Thomas laughed, so I turned it into a strip. Thomas is a great sounding board for my strip. If I can make him laugh, I know I've probably got something.

It's strips like this that make easily offended people write newspapers with comments such as, "Please tell me why it is funny when a sewing machine professes his love for Satan." I just think it's funny that I've made someone write a letter to a newspaper that includes the phrase "a sewing machine professes his love for Satan."

Just once I'd like to print someone's actual telephone number in a comic strip. If I ever do it, it will be the telephone number of my friend Emilio. He hates answering his phone, so the thought of it ringing day and night makes me laugh.

I think this was probably the most popular strip of 2007.

I love using swear squiggles in the phrase, "How the %#$# would I know?" The reason is that the phrase is only as dirty as you want it to be. For people with delicate sensibilities, it could simply be "hell" or even "heck." For people who talk more like my friends do, it could be a little more of the R-rated variety.

You can always expect at least one e-mail complaint when your strip in any way concerns suicide. Even if it's soap on a rope. It's utterly ridiculous. What am I supposed to say in response? "Thank you for your e-mail. In no way do I condone little bars of soap hanging themselves."

Whenever I see people with their collars up, I'm tempted to point it out to them like you would for someone who has a food stain on their shirt or food in their teeth, as if to say, "Your fashion sense is so offensive I'm assuming it's some sort of accident you'll want to fix."

Euripedes is a real frog, and he belongs to one of the salesmen for my syndicate, Ron O'Neal. The poor guy really has only one good eye. When Ron first told me about his frog's sad situation, I think the words that came out of my mouth were, "Awww. That poor frog," while the words in my head were, "Perfect for a comic strip."

If I remember right, I think I drew this strip for the sole purpose of being able to do the joke that appears in the next strip (the March 13, 2007, strip below).

After I drew these two strips, I let them sit a while because I didn't want to get a bunch of complaints about the stem cell debate, etc. Months later, I decided I wanted to do a story line where Rat clones himself, but I didn't know how to open the series. I went back to my shelf, saw these two strips, and thought they'd make a decent lead-in for the series. So I put the whole thing together like it was one story line.

This strip and the next one really work only if you know something about Rat's personality. One of the benefits of having done a strip for a few years is that the characters' personalities can become so well defined that you can just play off those reputations without having to set up the gags. Of course, for anyone reading the strip for the very first time, the joke would be almost entirely lost.

105

I don't know if this was a particularly funny strip, but I liked the image of the croc's wife on the beach. One funny image can sometimes save an otherwise mediocre strip. At least that's what I tell myself so I don't feel quite as crappy when I've just wasted four hours drawing and coloring a Sunday strip.

I thought it would be fun to somehow tie the crocs into this clone story line. I liked the way the croc's expression turned out.

The image of Rat in the second panel was taken from the 1968 Olympics protest where American athletes Tommie Smith and John Carlos raised their gloved fists like this on the medal stand. It was an extremely controversial act at the time.

All those smiling versions of Rat look so odd to me. Rat is just not meant to smile.

Originally, the clock was shouting, "Another CRAPPO day awaits," but any word that is a derivation of "crap" can cause problems. Hard to imagine a word like "crap" being at all controversial, but it can be on the comics page.

Because Bucky is so hard for me to draw, I just scanned this image of him out of a *Get Fuzzy* book and put it in my strip. That's what we in the business call "a real time-saver."

Pig drunk. I think this is a first for the strip.

Man, the problem with commenting on current events is that everyone forgets about the event later and then the strip no longer makes sense. Thus, for the ages, let me simply say that once there was this pop star named Britney Spears and one time she checked into rehab and shaved her head completely bald. So there. Now you future readers have no excuse for not understanding this joke.

I actually had to download this Britney Spears video onto my iPod to make sure I got Britney's clothes and stance right. (At least that's what I tell my friends when they ask me why I have Britney Spears on my iPod.)

The syndicate did not actually ask me to make any changes to this particular strip. I did it myself, knowing the strip could not go out with people's names in it.

The irony is that the syndicate *did* ask me to change this strip. In the last panel, Pig was originally staring straight at Britney, like he is in the second panel. The syndicate asked that he turn away from Britney in the last panel, as if to emphasize that once he realized she was not wearing underwear, he had the decency to turn away. Because I thought the strip worked either way, I changed it. Perhaps I'm getting soft in my old age.

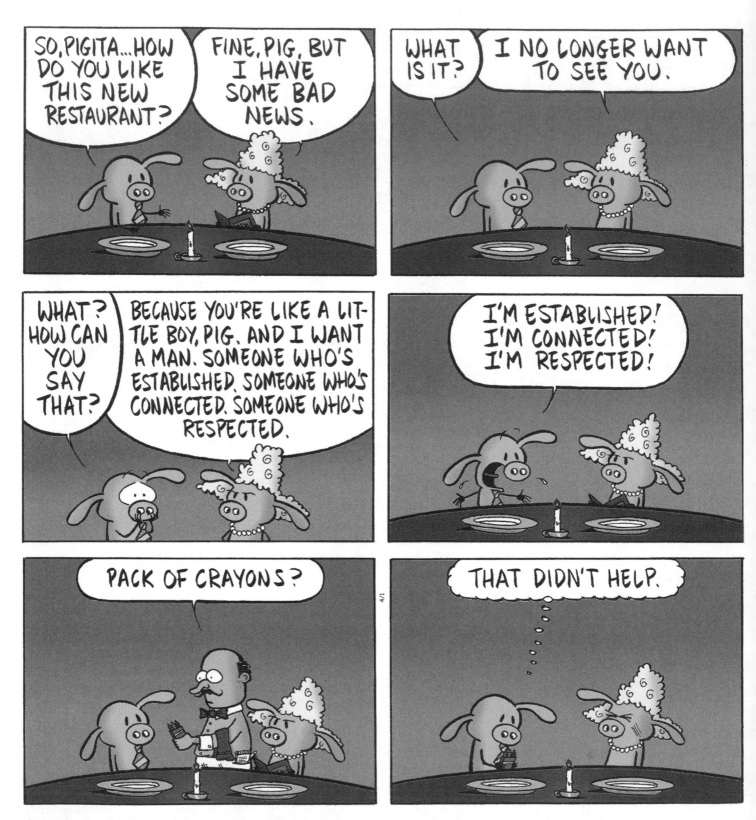

If a restaurant offers crayons, I always take them and color throughout the meal. It beats talking to the people I came to dinner with.

I recently forced myself to read a book on quantum physics, just to try and learn something new. I was confused by the middle of the first sentence and it all went downhill from there. The only thing I remember learning is that a parallel universe can theoretically be contained on the head of a needle. I don't really know what that means, but I am now more careful handling needles.

Every time I draw someone swinging a bat, I have to get out my old *Peanuts* books and see how to draw it.

I put Post-it notes everywhere to remind me of everything. I stick a ton of them on my computer monitor, telephone, and wallet. The problem now is that there are so many of them that my mind has blocked them all out. So I now need Post-it notes to remind me to look at my Post-it notes.

Any time you can do a panel where almost the entire thing is black, you've saved yourself that much drawing for the day. My recommendation for beginning cartoonists is to think of as many lights-out jokes as you can.

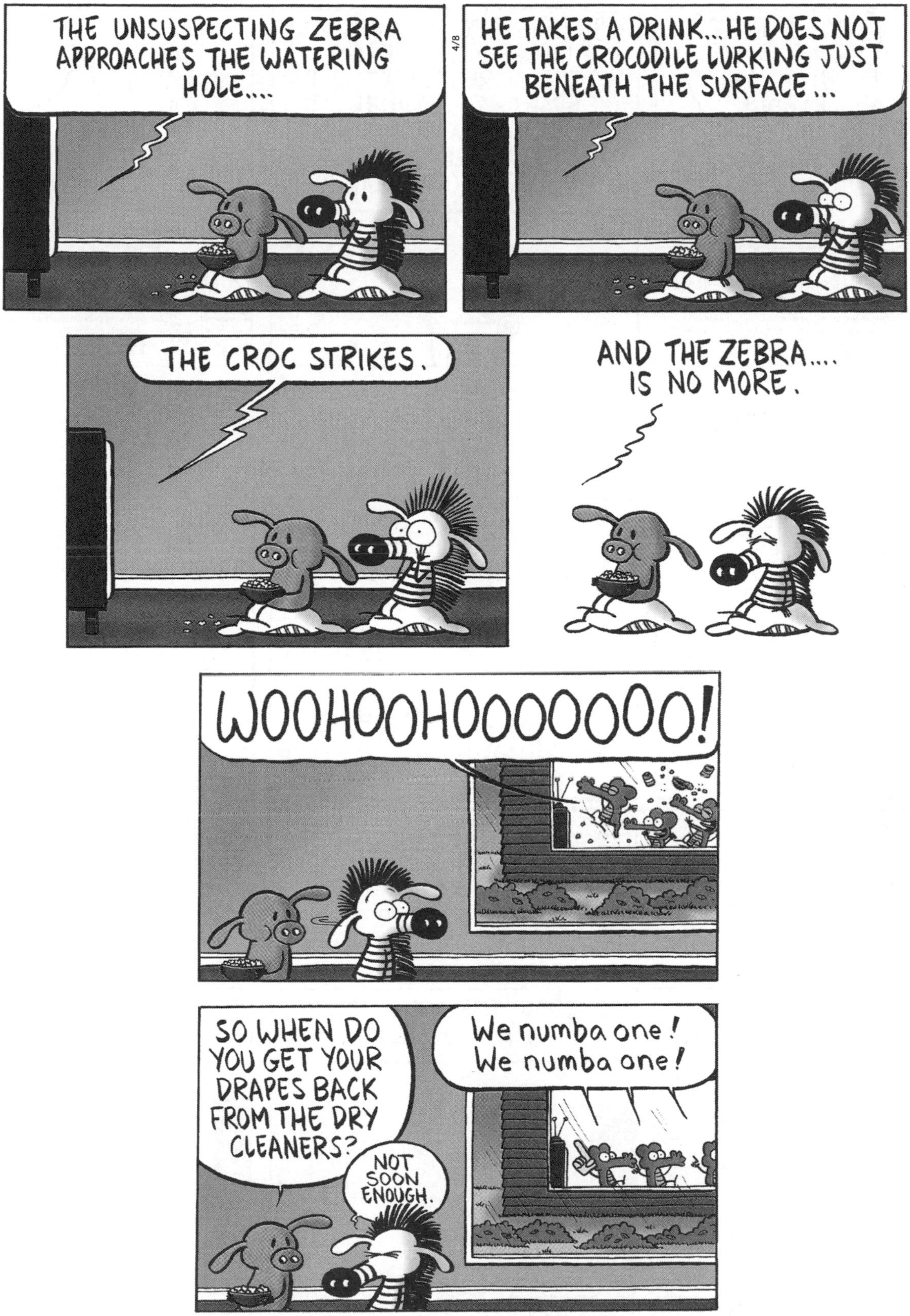
THE UNSUSPECTING ZEBRA APPROACHES THE WATERING HOLE....
4/8
HE TAKES A DRINK...HE DOES NOT SEE THE CROCODILE LURKING JUST BENEATH THE SURFACE...
THE CROC STRIKES.
AND THE ZEBRA.... IS NO MORE.
WOOHOOHOOOOOOO!
SO WHEN DO YOU GET YOUR DRAPES BACK FROM THE DRY CLEANERS?
We numba one! We numba one!
NOT SOON ENOUGH.

Look at the work that went into drawing the wood-grain paneling in the first and third panels. Why I felt it necessary to draw all that I cannot tell you. If you should ever meet me, lie and tell me it furthered your appreciation of the joke.

I'm Greek and thought everyone knew that Greek people sometimes broke plates at weddings. As it turned out, they did not. Perhaps my strip should contain footnotes and a handy glossary at the end.

Judging from the news shows I'm still seeing, no one was very afraid of Rat's frozen ham.

Pig can apparently speak Sumo Squirrelese.

I was surprised at the number of people who didn't know what "bupkiss" meant. It's a Yiddish word meaning "absolutely nothing."

To really mess with Larry, I thought it would be a good idea to not only make his son a vegetarian, but to also have him fall in love with someone Larry would consider prey. This doomed sort of *Romeo and Juliet* love story turned out to be really popular with readers.

My little tribute to Charles Schulz is on the pillow there.

Ricky Gervais (creator of the TV show *The Office*) once said that the key to comedic characters was the blind spot (i.e., the character thinks he's one thing, but is actually something quite different). So that's how I tried to design Larry and the rest of the crocs. They think they're skilled and knowledgeable predators, but they're really just idiots.

A rare reverse view of Rat in that second panel. It didn't come out that bad. I'm comforted by the notion that sometimes my drawing does not suck.

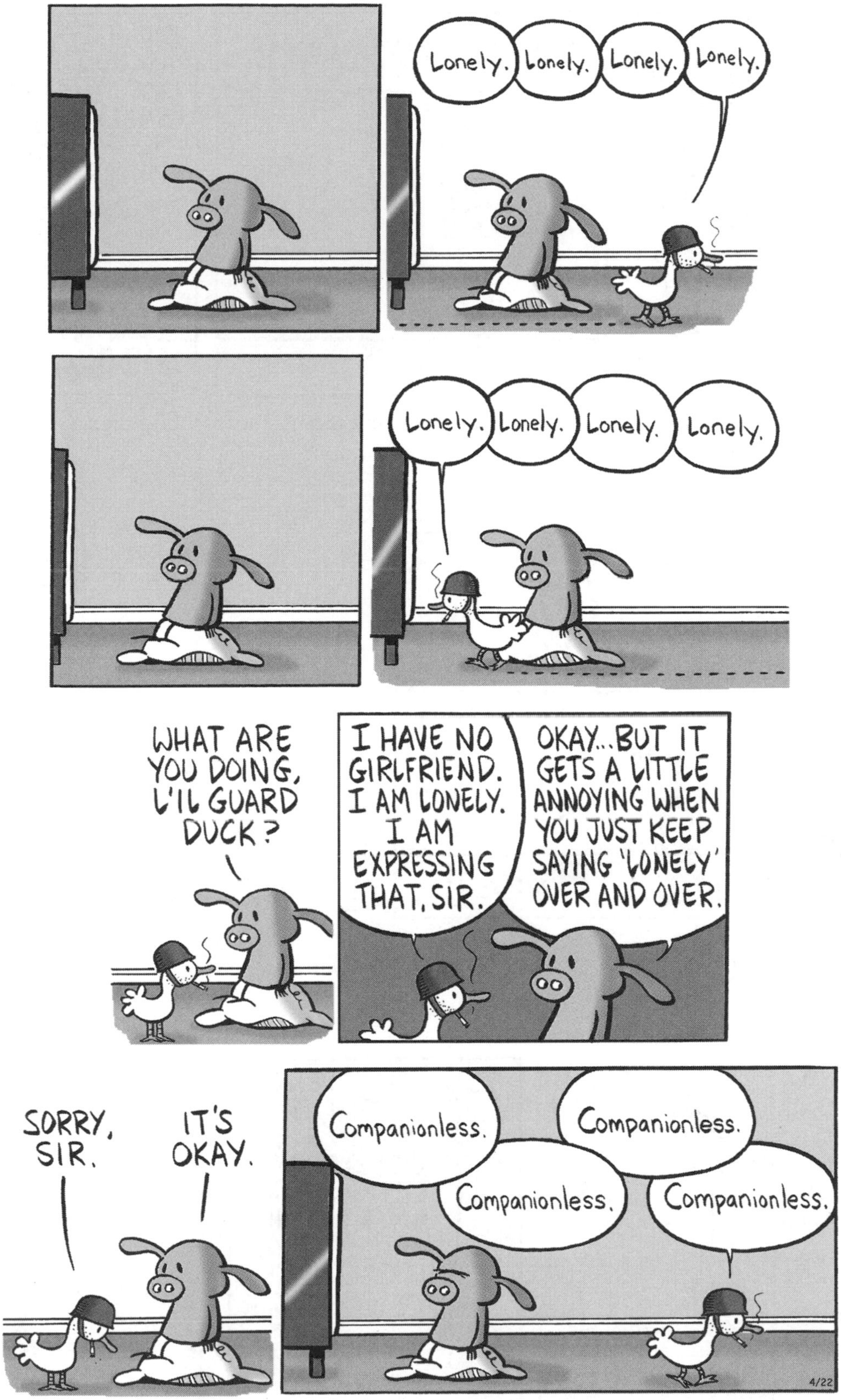
Lonely. Lonely. Lonely. Lonely.
Lonely. Lonely. Lonely. Lonely.
WHAT ARE YOU DOING, L'IL GUARD DUCK?
I HAVE NO GIRLFRIEND. I AM LONELY. I AM EXPRESSING THAT, SIR.
OKAY...BUT IT GETS A LITTLE ANNOYING WHEN YOU JUST KEEP SAYING 'LONELY' OVER AND OVER.
SORRY, SIR.
IT'S OKAY.
Companionless.
Companionless.
Companionless.
Companionless.
4/22

I named the little zebra after my grandmother Joy. She was my mom's mother. She died when I was five.

This particular sequence where Junior is separated from Joy turned out to be one of the most popular series I've ever done. I'm not sure what exactly it was, but it really seemed to resonate with some people.

One of only a small handful of *Pearls* strips that has absolutely no dialogue.

I think it's a good idea to sometimes do strips like this that are different from the general tone of *Pearls*. It shows that the strip is not *always* acerbic or about death.

Oops. Spoke too soon. One day after being so touching, I decided to throw a lawyer off a cliff. So much for the touchy-feely stuff.

I liked this image of the crocs so much that I made it the cover of the 2009 *Pearls* wall calendar.

Sadly, I really do this when people bore me. But it's not always the dwarfs I think about. Sometimes I try to list all the Canadian provinces.

A super-old strip that I put off running because I thought it was B-A-D bad. I still do. Don't look. Turn the page.

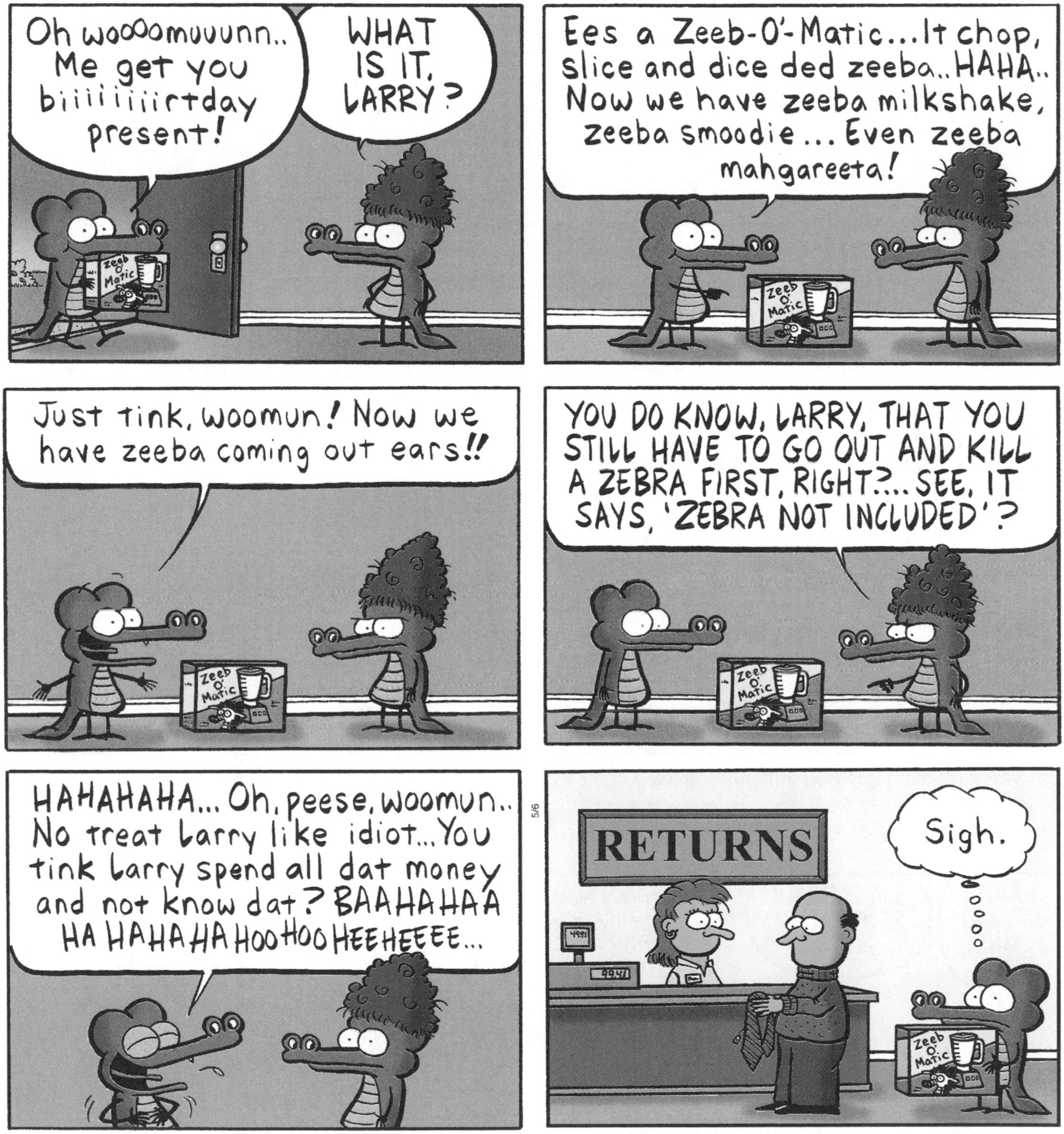
Oh wooOomuuunn.. Me get you biiiiiiirtday present!
WHAT IS IT, LARRY?
Zeeb O' Matic
Ees a Zeeb-O'-Matic...It chop, slice and dice ded zeeba..HAHA.. Now we have zeeba milkshake, zeeba smoodie... Even zeeba mahgareeta!
Just tink, woomun! Now we have zeeba coming out ears!!
YOU DO KNOW, LARRY, THAT YOU STILL HAVE TO GO OUT AND KILL A ZEBRA FIRST, RIGHT?...SEE, IT SAYS, 'ZEBRA NOT INCLUDED'?
HAHAHAHA... Oh, peese, woomun.. No treat Larry like idiot...You tink Larry spend all dat money and not know dat? BAAHAHAA HA HAHAHA HOOHOO HEEHEEEE...
RETURNS
Sigh.

This came from something I vaguely remember doing when I was a little kid. I bought something that I thought was a vacuum cleaner for my mom. I thought it was a vacuum cleaner because there was a vacuum cleaner on the side of the box. I couldn't believe my luck when I saw it because it was just a few dollars, something I could actually afford. As it turned out, it was just a vacuum cleaner attachment. When my mom opened it, there was a look of great confusion on her face.

I actually got this idea from Bil Keane, the creator of *Family Circus*. I was at his house once, and he told me a story about this time he had to fill out a government form and answer a question about whether he would ever advocate the overthrow of the U.S. government by force or violence. He chose violence. I thought it was so funny that I wanted to come up with my own version of the joke.

This was an amazingly popular strip. I think it came to me while driving somewhere with my son. Whenever I get an idea while driving, I tell the joke to my son and he writes it down for me. Wary of always having to write stuff down, his first question is always the same, "It's not a Sunday, is it?"

Another really old couple of strips that I put off running for a while. I'm not sure why though. I sorta like them.

I wanted to use the name of a real Ultimate Fighting Championship fighter here, but I was afraid he would take offense at the notion that his wife was loose, in which case I might actually share the fate of Angry Bob. So I thought better of it.

Rachel McAdams is in a movie called *The Notebook*. On a plane flight to Japan, I watched it three times and cried each time. This is very embarrassing, so do *not* tell anyone else I said this.

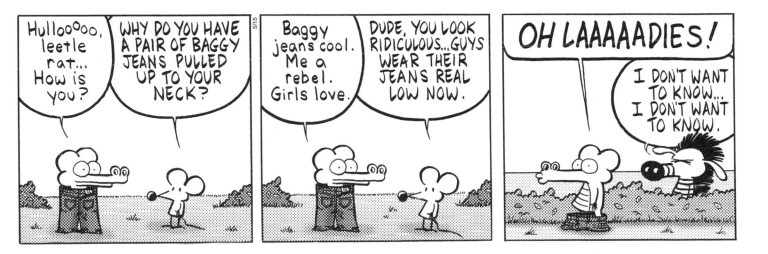

After these strips appeared, some readers wanted the Deaths to become regular characters. I'd do it, but those robes are too hard to draw. Now if the new next-door neighbor had been Sticky the Stick-Figure Man, it'd be a different story.

This strip arose from a sketch of Pig in my notebook where Pig was wearing this inflatable raft. I liked the way he looked, so I created a strip around it. Sometimes a strip will generate itself from a random doodle like that.

Saturday = Place to hide the poop jokes.

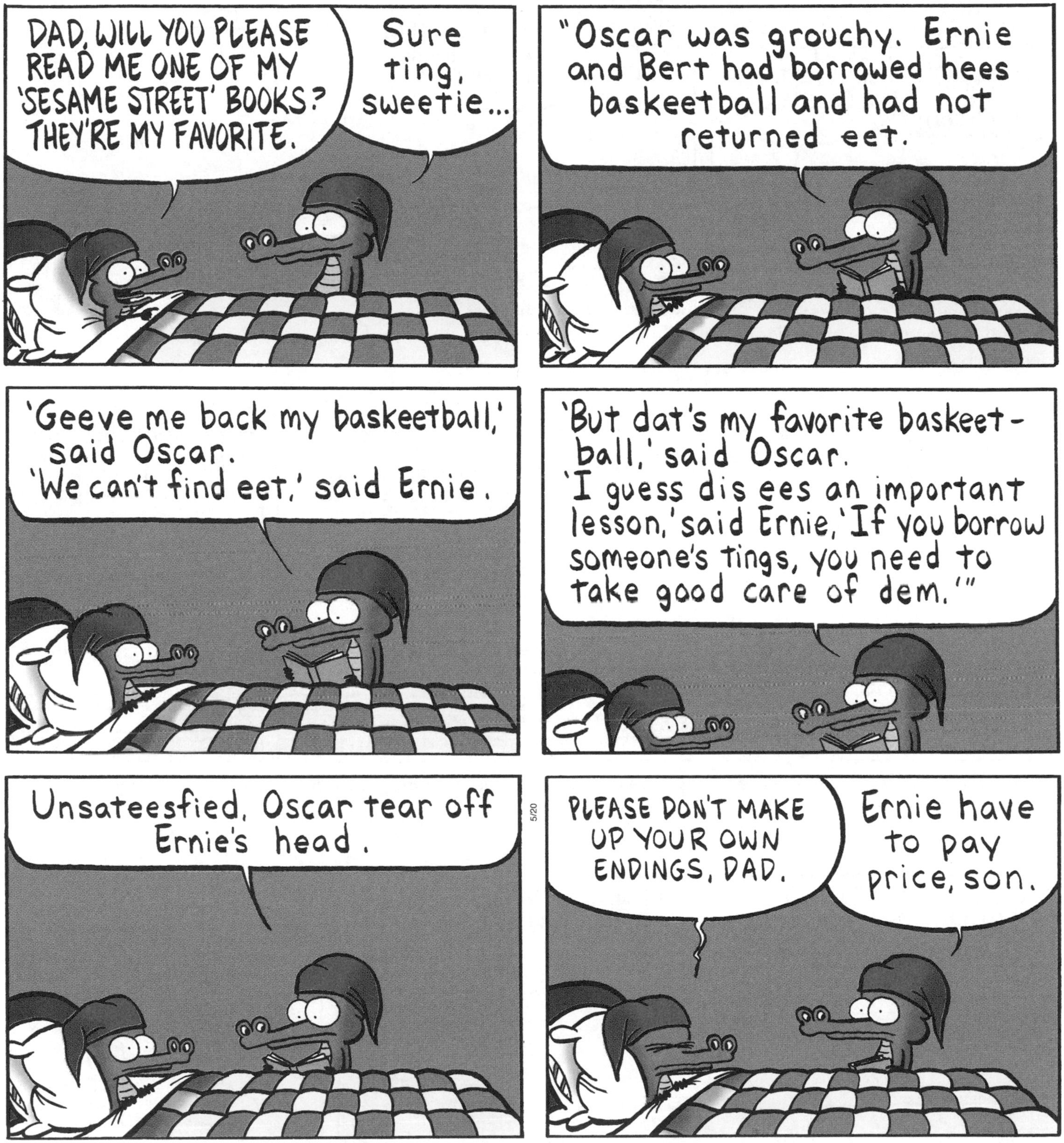

DAD, WILL YOU PLEASE READ ME ONE OF MY 'SESAME STREET' BOOKS? THEY'RE MY FAVORITE.
Sure ting, sweetie...
"Oscar was grouchy. Ernie and Bert had borrowed hees baskeetball and had not returned eet.
'Geeve me back my baskeetball,' said Oscar.
'We can't find eet,' said Ernie.
'But dat's my favorite baskeet-ball,' said Oscar.
'I guess dis ees an important lesson,' said Ernie, 'If you borrow someone's tings, you need to take good care of dem.'"
Unsateesfied, Oscar tear off Ernie's head.
5/20
PLEASE DON'T MAKE UP YOUR OWN ENDINGS, DAD.
Ernie have to pay price, son.

When you can't draw chameleons and you can't draw blenders, it's a bad idea to write strips where chameleons become blenders.

This is how I comfort friends. When I say "friends," I use that term loosely, as I don't actually have any.

Stephan's Guide to Drawing Cheese: 1) Draw a box; 2) Fill it with holes; 3) Have someone in the strip call it "cheese."

All I remember about these next two strips was that I was on vacation when they ran, and when I got back, I saw from my e-mail that they did not generate a big reaction. That made me sad. But then I told myself that all of you must have been on vacation, too.

This joke sounded funny in my head. Then I saw it on paper.

This strip was based on the R.E.M. song, "It's the End of the World as We Know It." Half of my readers knew the song and half did not. This latter group was therefore very confused. More important, the strip got the attention of an executive at R.E.M.'s record label, who said the band would like to have the original. I sent the strip to them and in exchange, got a whole mess of R.E.M. CDs and DVDs, as well as one of Michael Stipe's lyric sheets that he had once used on stage. I need to try this trick with U2.

A rare, facedown pose of Pig. That makes up for the poorly drawn tree.

This strip marked the introduction of Zebra's *other* next-door neighbors, the Lions.

I have no real comment to make regarding this strip, but I feel bad going three straight strips without a comment. So here I'll just say hello and tell you that my favorite color is blue.

I didn't know how to draw a concrete statue of Guard Duck and make it actually look like concrete, so I called Rick Kirkman (cocreator of *Baby Blues*) and asked him if he could sketch it for me. He e-mailed me his drawing and I pretty much just copied it. So my advice here is that if you ever have trouble drawing something, call Rick Kirkman.

I think I was influenced by Groucho Marx in writing the Guard Duck's lines here. It is amazing to watch clips of Groucho and see how fast his comedic mind worked.

As I think I've admitted before, I watch a lot of MTV's *The Real World*. Given that I'm now forty, I suppose that's kind of embarrassing. Not as embarrassing as crying during three straight viewings of *The Notebook*, but still, embarrassing.

Alright, while I'm in a confessional mood, I gotta admit that I absolutely love those Rick Steves travel shows on PBS. I think I was secretly hoping he'd see this strip and offer me a two-month all-expenses-paid trip to Europe. It did not happen.

I purposely drew Zebra eating a lobster here to show that he's a bit of a hypocrite. While he doesn't want the crocodiles eating him, he has no trouble eating other living creatures. Fortunately, he's just a cartoon character and doesn't know I dissed him.

I have never seen even one minute of *Desperate Housewives*, but I am fairly certain it is a TV show.

For those of you who don't know, *All the President's Men* chronicles many of the illegal things done by President Richard Nixon and his administration. It's a great book but not one you'd want to use as a primer on good government.

It's odd how you can't say "screwed" or "sucked" on the comics page but for some reason "hosed" is okay.

This strip marked the first appearance of Andy. I meant for this to be a one-time-only appearance, but he resonated with people, so I brought him back later as a semiregular character.

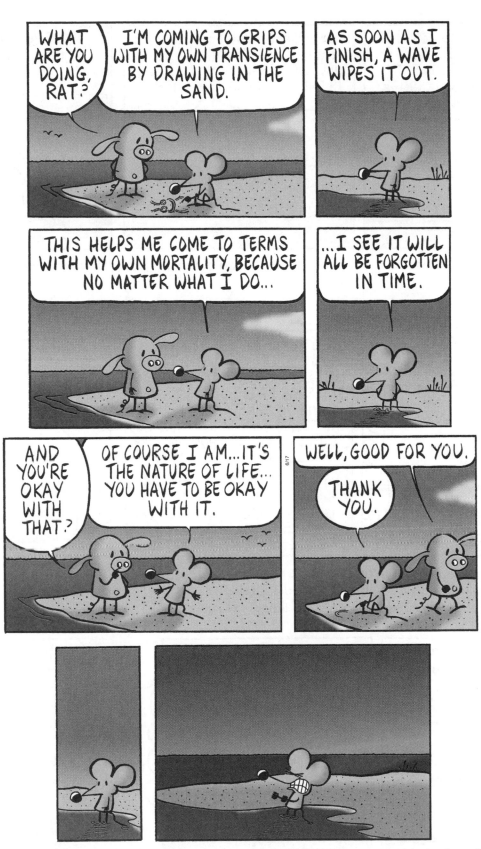

A rare, semiserious strip for *Pearls*. I like to do these once or maybe twice a year. More than that and you risk being called *For Better or For Worse*.

This is another strip that arose from a random doodle. I had drawn Rat as a clown and liked the way he looked, so I built a strip around it.

Okay, can I just say that that stupid little car took me about an hour to draw. Cars are just murder for me. I'm hoping that the whole world's transportation needs transition to something easier to draw, like maybe giant balloons attached to people's heads. I can draw those.

Alright fine, I cut and pasted this group of people a couple times. But if you look really carefully, you'll see that I changed the mouth on the bald guy standing next to Guard Duck. I should get some points for that.

This is a parody of the famous photo taken of Richard Nixon as he left the White House for the final time. Despite resigning in disgrace, he turned on the steps of the helicopter and made the "V" for victory sign with both hands.

There's that #&$% car again.

I don't know if this was a great strip, but I was proud that I was the first cartoonist to merge a movie about gang life in south-central L.A. (*Menace II Society*) with beloved cartoon idol Dennis the Menace.

You can't go wrong basing comedy around sporks. Sporks are the wacky uncle of the utensil family.

This turned out to be a really popular strip, probably one of the most popular of the year.

Because I can't say "cash for sex" on the comics page, I have to talk in code and say "cash for affection." Perhaps one day I will reveal my whole secret code to you.

I liked Rat's line in the second panel ("Doing right is to making money what deflating tires is to riding a bicycle"). I guess that's sort of bad form to say I liked something I wrote. But that doesn't stop me.

I frequently draw while wearing just my boxers. So when the doorbell rings, I start to walk toward the front door wearing nothing but boxers. Then a little voice in my head says, "Stop. You are not wearing pants."

I really liked the phrase on the newspaper, "From altar boy to altered boy." Again, it's very bad form to praise your own writing.

When I took my kids to Mexico last summer, I told them that *"Donde esta el queso de mi padre"* was the most important phrase they needed to learn. When I told them what it meant, they just stared at me. It's a sad thing when your own kids find you obnoxious.

This was a very popular strip. Had I known it was going to be so popular, I would not have run it on a holiday.

This generated many complaints and letters to the editor. The complaint was that the crocodile was killed. At first I didn't understand, because the crocs are always being killed. The difference here? The moment of death is shown. Subtle distinction, but it made a huge difference in reader response. Made me want to do it more often.

I e-mailed this to Brian Walker before it ran. Brian is the son of Mort Walker, the creator of *Beetle Bailey*. Brian is also one of the cocreators of *Hi and Lois*. I was a little worried about what the Walkers would think of it, but Brian said he loved it. He was a great sport.

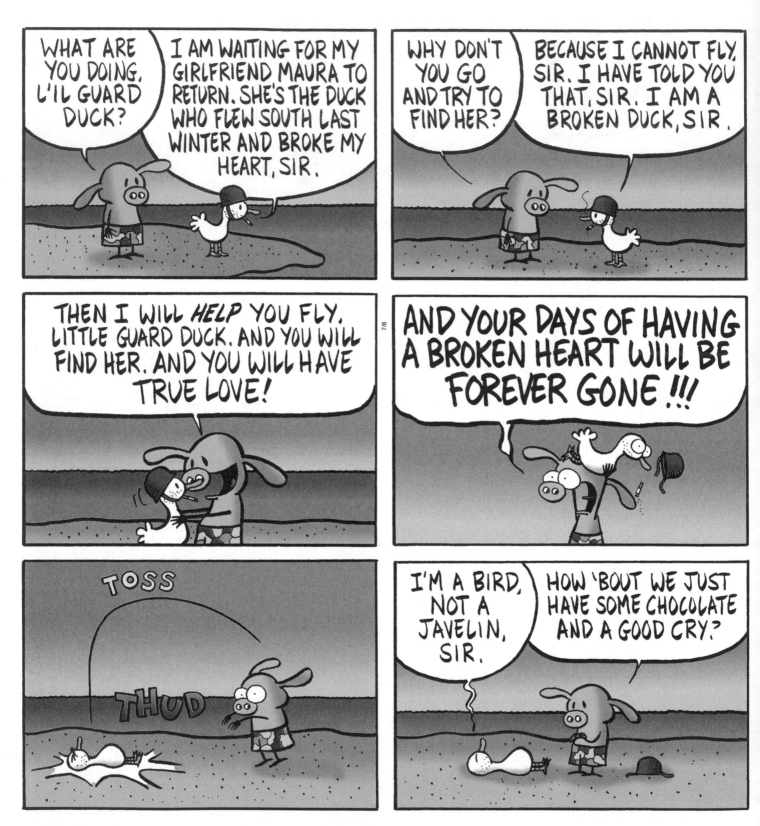

Oddly, the color pattern on Pig's shorts seems to change in every panel. Perhaps they are magical.

I DON'T UNDERSTAND IT. I'M MAKING ALL THIS MONEY PUBLISHING A TABLOID, BUT I'M STILL NOT HAPPY.

AH...AND WHAT LESSON DOES THAT TEACH YOU?

THAT I MUST NOT BE MAKING ENOUGH MONEY.

WRONG LESSON.

WELL, I'M OFF TO RUIN SOME MORE LIVES.

HEY THERE, RAT...DID YOU SEE MY NEW STEREO?

WHAT KIND IS IT?

Heeeeey, LITTLE COFFEE MUG... DOING ANYTHING FRIDAY?...THE WIFE'S OUT OF TOWN AND——

YOUR WIFE'S RIGHT HERE. CLARENCE!

HIGH INFIDELITY.

This strip didn't really work. Part of the problem was that it wasn't clear it was the speakers themselves talking. Since voices often come out of speakers, it could have been a CD playing or a radio station or something. Now when an oversight like this occurs, the easiest thing for a cartoonist to do is to blame his editor. So I shall do that.

YOU KNOW, I KNOW YOUR WIFE DOES YOUR HUNTING FOR YOU, BUT COULD YOU HUNT IF YOU HAD TO?

Oh yeah...But that's not a big deal... All it takes is a willingness to kill and a minimum level of competence.

Me hate you lots.

I think this was my attempt to explain Zebra's "next-door neighbor" situation. The way I've haphazardly developed it, he has three next-door neighbors: 1) the fraternity of crocodiles; 2) the family of crocodiles (Larry, his wife, and son); and 3) the lions. This is sort of a problem, though, because most people think you can only have two next-door neighbors, the ones on the left side of your house and the ones on the right side of your house. So I hedged it here by placing one of the neighbors (Larry) *behind* Zebra's house. Ohhh, the cleverness of me.

I actually tried to spill liquid on one of my drawings to see if I could achieve this effect, but the spill barely affected the artwork. So I had to do this little effect on the computer.

I got HBO the day of the *Sopranos* finale just so I could see the finale live. In the last scene, the screen goes totally black. Thus, you don't know what happens to the main character. You just have to guess. I, of course, started swearing like an insane lunatic because I figured the cable box I had just installed had somehow become disconnected.

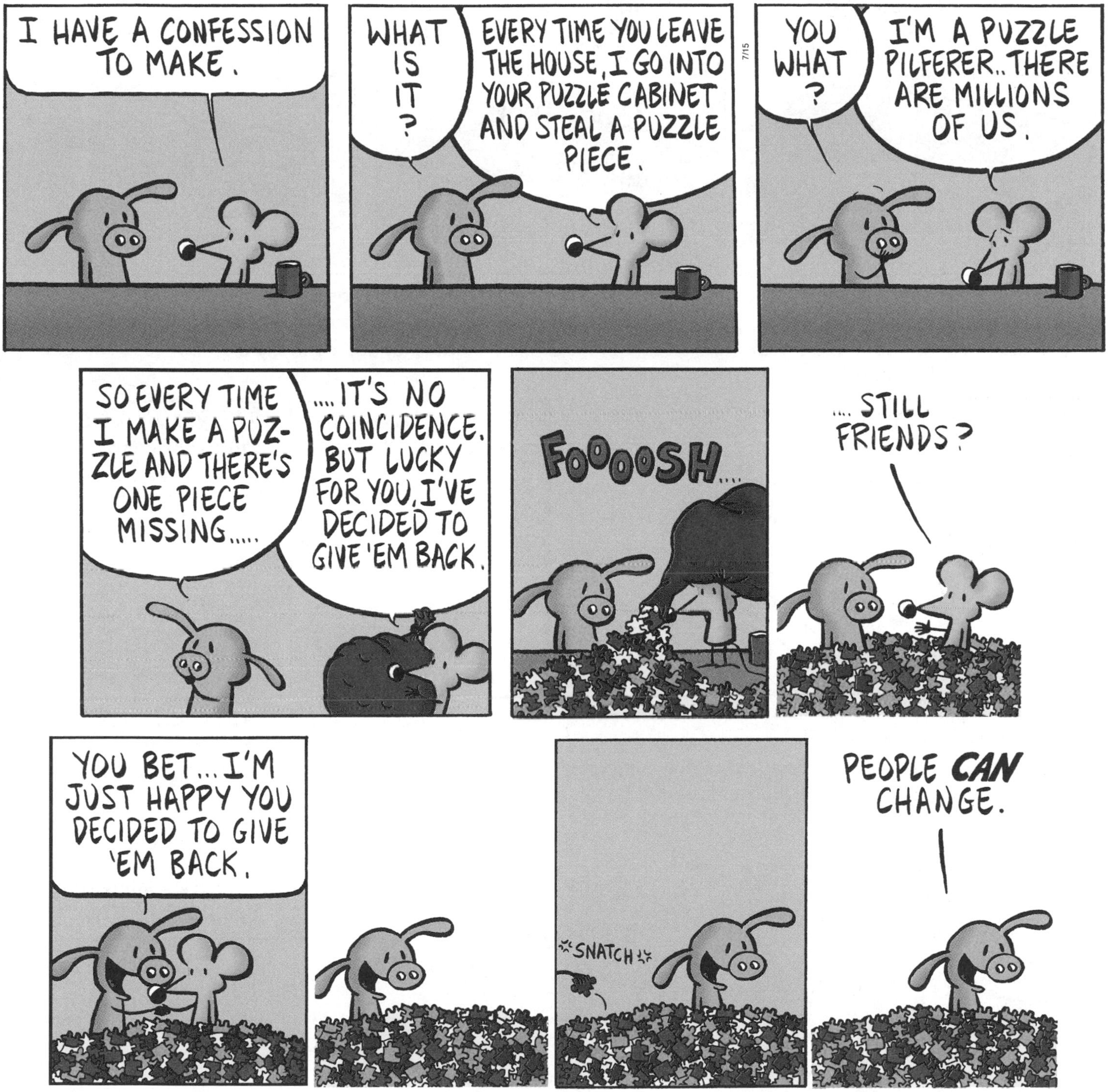
I HAVE A CONFESSION TO MAKE.
WHAT IS IT?
EVERY TIME YOU LEAVE THE HOUSE, I GO INTO YOUR PUZZLE CABINET AND STEAL A PUZZLE PIECE.
7/15
YOU WHAT?
I'M A PUZZLE PILFERER.. THERE ARE MILLIONS OF US.
SO EVERY TIME I MAKE A PUZ-ZLE AND THERE'S ONE PIECE MISSING.....
....IT'S NO COINCIDENCE. BUT LUCKY FOR YOU, I'VE DECIDED TO GIVE 'EM BACK.
FOOOOSH....
.... STILL FRIENDS?
YOU BET... I'M JUST HAPPY YOU DECIDED TO GIVE 'EM BACK.
SNATCH
PEOPLE CAN CHANGE.

One strange rule of the comics is that you cannot use the word "hell" in phrases such as "Hell no," or "Leave me the hell alone." If you do, you'll get a number of complaints. But if are using "hell" literally (i.e., as the actual place mentioned in the Bible), no one complains at all. At least that has been my experience. Why the distinction? Hell if I know.

I am Goat here. One day I learned what the "zip" in "zip code" stood for and I went around telling everyone I know.

It is rather strange how anonymity often brings out the worst in us. When I say "us," I mean "people other than me." I, for one, am kind to others 24/7.

This was a really old strip which for one reason or another I didn't run until years after I had drawn it. The problem, though, was that it dated back to the days when Zebra only *heard* about what the predators did to his family back home, and in the intervening years, the predators, such as the crocs and the lions, had actually moved in next door to him. Thus, when the strip finally appeared, the premise was sort of outdated. Once again I shall take the high road here and blame my editor.

Somebody I know (who shall remain nameless) asked if I could include the name of her and her husband in a strip. I did. And it was in this strip. I showed it to her before it ran and she almost started crying. The reason? She and her husband had been having some problems (which she thought I knew about, but I didn't) and she figured this was my commentary on their marriage. I immediately changed the names. Ever since, I've been very wary of including the names of people I know in the comic. You never know how they'll interpret it.

Connie the Judgmental Cow was pretty popular. I did not name her after anybody I know.

Every time I see this strip, I cringe, because something is off. I think I had a funny idea at one point and somehow blew it. I apologize for any inconvenience it may cause you.

Man, this was a strange strip. And for me, that's saying something.

I seem to have done many a strip where the characters or people are sitting in boxes. I think it's because they're easy to draw. After eight years of doing the strip, it's the only shape I appear to have a handle on.

More boxes. My goodness, it's out of control.

I always enjoy slamming my old profession. (For those of you who don't know, I was a lawyer for nine years before becoming a cartoonist.)

I kind of regretted doing this strip, because Junior never wore pants again. Then again, who am I to start worrying about plot consistency? I bring back dead characters by saying they "un-died."

I liked this strip. It's a throwback to how the strip originally was. Just Rat and Pig talking. It's pretty much all I ever drew in the first couple years of syndication.

Another strip referencing the way *The Sopranos* ended. I was really hoping David Chase would contact me and invite me to his house to tell me how the series *really* ended. But it didn't happen. For the record, though, I'm gonna say that I'm one of those fans that think Tony was killed.

This was an attempt to mimic the success I had with the crocodile in the water cooler strip (the March 5, 2007, strip). But it wasn't as well received. I almost never succeed when I try to play off the success of an earlier strip.

If you're a cartoonist, and you're stuck for ideas, do a strip where something violent happens to a mime. It's instant comedy, and no one ever complains. I suppose mimes would like to, but they can't talk.

Ego-Man was very popular, much more popular than I expected.

I got this idea after visiting the writer Jack London's old house in Glen Ellen, California. He was very big on living life to the fullest and not worrying about dying. As a result, he lived a life filled with adventure and died at the young age of forty. I say "young" because I'm forty now.

This was the beginning of a big, long, multiweek experiment in *Pearls*. I purposely wrote a whole bunch of totally independent story lines (the lawyer one, the astronaut one, the Segway one, and the Bil Keane/Jeffy one) and then tried to somehow tie them all together. It was sort of a challenge to myself. I don't know how well it worked, but I enjoyed trying to do it.

These lawyer strips went over pretty big with the members of my old profession.

This was probably the most popular strip of the lawyer series. People liked the "scratch and ween" line.

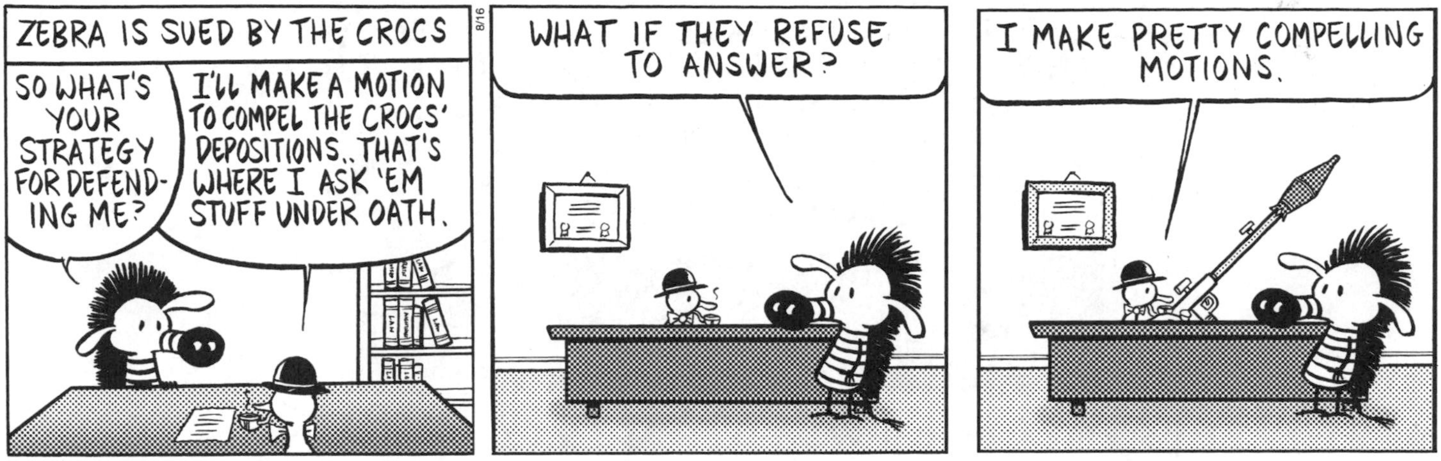
ZEBRA IS SUED BY THE CROCS
8/16
SO WHAT'S YOUR STRATEGY FOR DEFENDING ME?
I'LL MAKE A MOTION TO COMPEL THE CROCS' DEPOSITIONS..THAT'S WHERE I ASK 'EM STUFF UNDER OATH.
WHAT IF THEY REFUSE TO ANSWER?
I MAKE PRETTY COMPELLING MOTIONS.

Why the heck did I draw the Duck's desk so tiny? I'm sure I must have had a reason. If you know what it was, please let me know.

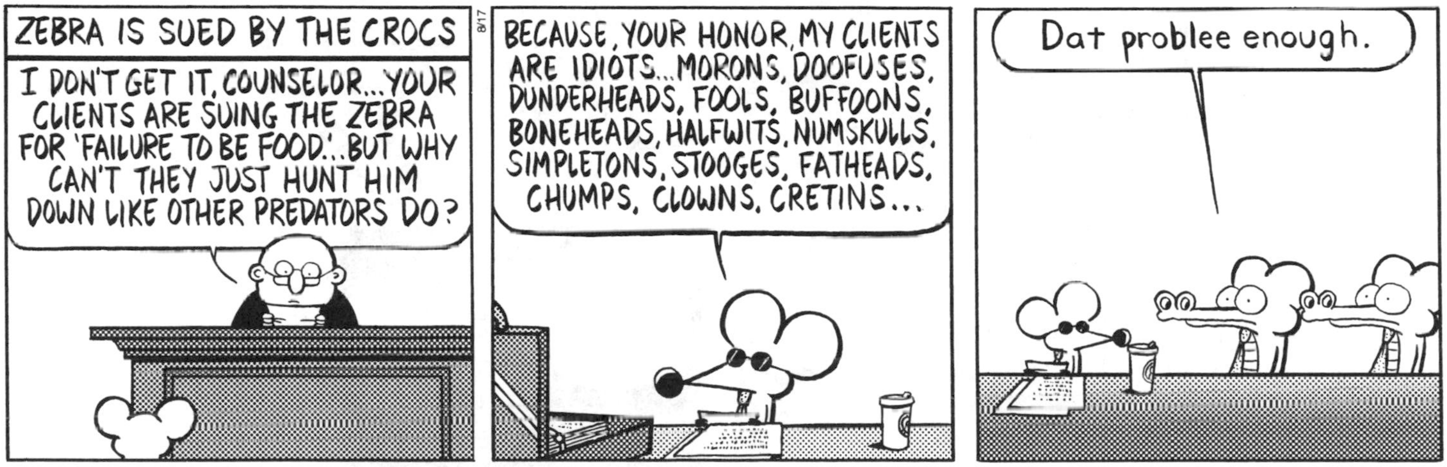
ZEBRA IS SUED BY THE CROCS
8/17
I DON'T GET IT, COUNSELOR...YOUR CLIENTS ARE SUING THE ZEBRA FOR 'FAILURE TO BE FOOD.'..BUT WHY CAN'T THEY JUST HUNT HIM DOWN LIKE OTHER PREDATORS DO?
BECAUSE, YOUR HONOR, MY CLIENTS ARE IDIOTS...MORONS, DOOFUSES, DUNDERHEADS, FOOLS, BUFFOONS, BONEHEADS, HALFWITS, NUMSKULLS, SIMPLETONS, STOOGES, FATHEADS, CHUMPS, CLOWNS, CRETINS...
Dat problee enough.

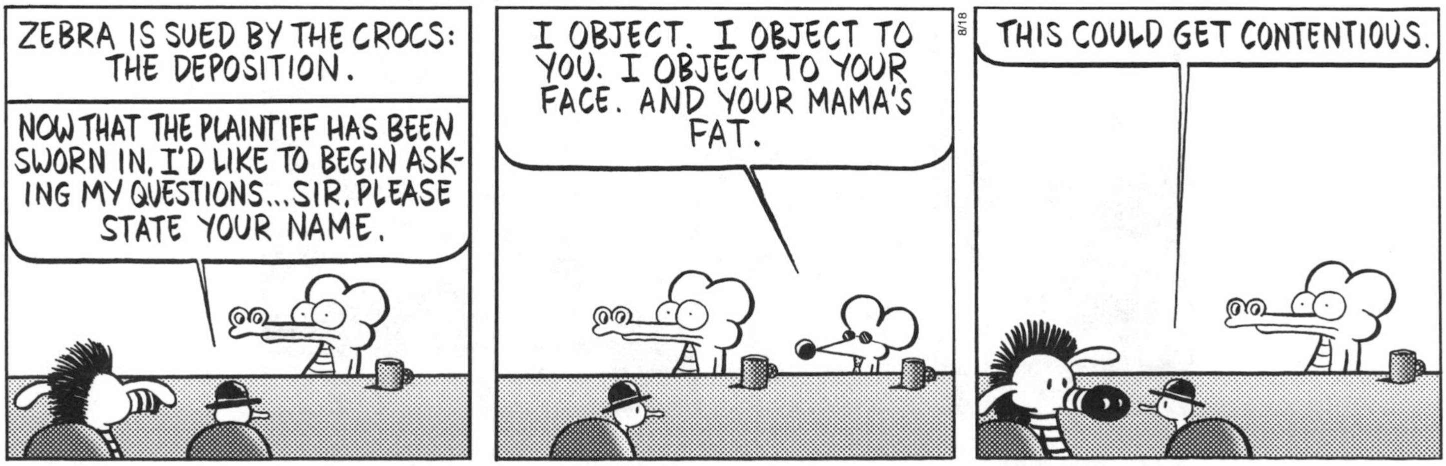
ZEBRA IS SUED BY THE CROCS: THE DEPOSITION.
8/18
NOW THAT THE PLAINTIFF HAS BEEN SWORN IN, I'D LIKE TO BEGIN ASKING MY QUESTIONS...SIR, PLEASE STATE YOUR NAME.
I OBJECT. I OBJECT TO YOU. I OBJECT TO YOUR FACE. AND YOUR MAMA'S FAT.
THIS COULD GET CONTENTIOUS.

In my career as an attorney, I probably did around two hundred or so of these depositions where you sit there and ask the witness a whole bunch of questions under oath. And believe me, some of them were almost as bad as this. The worst was one time when the opposing counsel threw a microphone at me and left. I knew I must have asked a good question.

This strip went over very big. Apparently, there are a lot of people out there who can't stand serial strips. By the way, that phone took me longer to draw than the entire rest of the strip.

When you're a lawyer, you have to account for every minute of your working day. Billable hours are the key to your survival. Now I sit around in my underwear and doodle. Big improvement.

This was a reference to that story in the news where a female astronaut was accused of driving from Texas to Florida to attack a woman who she thought was a rival for the affections of a male astronaut. She was said to have worn a diaper on the drive so she didn't have to stop and use restrooms along the way. Speaking as a cartoonist who is always on the lookout for material, stories like that are what you call "a freebie."

That's quite a strange-looking car. That's what you get when you're a cartoonist who can't really draw cars.

I'm not sure why it is that Pig is wearing a full suit while the crocs have on only ties. I can tell you from my days as a lawyer that most courts do require pants.

174

When I was twelve or so, I had a friend in Malibu, California, who had one of these spear guns. One day when I was visiting him, he demonstrated it by shooting it into a phone book. It went right through the phone book and made a hole in his bedroom wall. It scared the bejesus out of me. I think that fear was probably the unconscious genesis of this strip.

I don't know what it is about those Segways, but they really make me laugh. The person standing on them just looks so goofy. I've always wanted to write a horror screenplay where the killer was some old person riding around on one of those things. Not sure what that says about me, but it probably doesn't bode well for my screenwriting aspirations.

Ah, see how I've cleverly interwoven the astronaut story line with this Segway story line? I'd like to think that makes up for that crappy crocodile strip in July.

After this strip appeared, a newspaper in Arizona wrote an article about how my comic strip had mentioned the town of Surprise. It contained a quote by a spokesperson for the city, who said something about how he liked the reference but was disappointed that the strip had just shown some cacti, instead of some new buildings the city was proud of. He apparently thought I had the drawing abilities of a normal cartoonist.

You can never go wrong shoehorning an already convoluted story line into a *Family Circus* parody.

I had drawn Bil Keane's characters into the strip before, but I had never actually drawn Bil Keane. Notice how I put him in a circle, a subtle reference to the circle his comic appears in. So subtle, in fact, that I myself didn't realize it until just now, when I was writing this comment.

177

See, if I only have to draw a small fraction of a car (like just the back fender), I can make it look almost like a car.

When this strip and the September 1, 2007, strip appeared, I called Bil Keane and asked him if he personally had ever appeared in a comic strip before. He said yes. I then added, "But have you ever appeared as a sociopathic murderer?" He thought about it for a moment and said, "No, I guess I haven't."

I was worried about the dialogue flow of this strip (i.e., whether people would know to read Rat's line, then Jeffy's, then Rat's, etc.). But I guess it was understandable.

I don't know about you, but my Slinkys never lasted longer than a day. After that, they almost always got a kink in them. I had a rough childhood.

Okay, strange confession time. I sometimes walk through graveyards listening to my iPod. It's really relaxing. I have yet to run into any zombies.

Bil Keane occasionally asks for some of the *Family Circus* parody strips I do. I believe this was one he asked for. So I sent it to him.

"It's 'Jeffy,' not 'Jiffy.'"

So here I've connected the *Family Circus* story line back up with the original lawyer story line, clearly establishing this as the most convoluted plot I've ever created in the strip.

"Whatever."

I once asked the real Jeff Keane (the son of Bil Keane and the model for "Jeffy") what he thought of how I drew Jeffy. Jeff currently draws *Family Circus*. He said it was good but that Jeffy's head was too long from front to back. To heck with him. What does he know?

I like portraying Jeffy as a backstabbing, murderous traitor. I'd like to see more of that in *Family Circus*.

Because I thought squeezing four or five story lines into one was not enough, I thought I'd throw in a little Ego-Man too.

Whenever I draw a character with an angel or devil over their shoulder, it reminds of that famous scene from the movie *Animal House* where Pinto had that angel and devil yelling contradictory advice to him. That movie had a big impact on me as a little kid. Looking back on it, I probably saw it at too young an age. I think the father of my friend with the spear gun took me to see it. Wonder if he ever found out about the hole his kid made in the bedroom wall.

I believe this was the only really extended series I've ever done that focused just on Goat. I realized I had never developed him as a character and wanted to change that.

Even though I drew this "Goat goes home" series in March, 2007, it appeared in newspapers two weeks after I traveled to a big family wedding in Southern California. To my family, I'm sure it appeared that the series was based on my recent experience. It wasn't. But my timing could have been better.

This was based on my Yiayia (Greek for "grandmother"). She fed me like this every time I came to her house and was constantly reminding me of how skinny I was. I could have been three hundred pounds and still she would have told me that.

And this was my tribute to my grandfather, Paris Tripodes. He died in 1962, six years before I was born. I've always wished I could have met him. If you look at the cover of the last treasury, *The Crass Menagerie,* his photo appears on the bookshelf.

This is something that always bothers me. You see a kid with their parent in the park, and the parent spends the whole time on the cell phone. It always breaks my heart.

I just wanted to make the point here that sometimes you return home, and you don't know who's changed, you or your family. Again, it could have been timed better so that it didn't appear just two weeks after I saw everyone.

Wow, it's not every day you see the same pose cut and pasted three times. Oh wait, I made a tiny little change to Goat's eyes in the last panel. Phew. That makes me feel better.

Unfortunate Piece of Timing Number Two. Alright, first I do a series that appears to be making fun of all the relatives I had just seen at a family wedding two weeks prior. And what do I do next? I mock the wedding itself. A wedding in which I was the best man. Once again, these strips were done many months before my visit, but it didn't matter. It looked bad.

On the list of things I cannot draw, wedding dresses are right there next to cars.

This strip marked the introduction of Snuffles the cat. At first, he was just supposed to be a cute little cat. His personality would change over time.

For some reason, all three of these were popular strips. I was really worried about them, because I couldn't tell if they were any good or not. Heck, I never know.

I was most worried about this one, because I wasn't sure how clear it was that that was supposed to be cat poop in there. By the way, "poop" is a word you can't say on the comics page. At least not without drawing complaints. So I will make up for it here. Poop. Poop. Poop.

Little did I know until after this strip was published that "pooter" has various slang meanings, none of which I can repeat here. Good thing newspaper editors didn't know them either.

This is one of my favorite Danny Donkey strips. By the way, that's me at the head of the line in the fourth panel.

There really *are* lilac festivals. And people go to them. I wonder if they get together in gangs and fight daffodil lovers.

This was based on the famous incident in 2007 when U.S. senator Larry Craig was arrested for "lewd conduct" in an airport bathroom. The undercover officer that arrested Craig said that Craig rubbed his foot against his under the bathroom stall wall. According to the police report, Craig stated he had not done it intentionally. It was just that he had a "wide stance."

Is there really such a thing as a sea squirrel? I'm gonna have to look that up.

That's the name of the high school I attended on the yearbook there. That's the same high school that awarded me "Most Obnoxious" when I graduated in 1986. I *earned* it.

Strangely, real pens don't make "write write write" sounds when you use them. I've used some artistic license there.

This was a really popular strip, and it generated a huge reaction. For those of you who don't know the original line, it was from President Franklin Delano Roosevelt: "The only thing we have to fear is fear itself."

This was sort of based on our own hamsters, one of which would just go to town on his squeaky wheel in the middle of the night. I finally had to go downstairs one night and take the wheel out of his cage because I just couldn't sleep. He stared at me bitterly. I'm fairly certain I heard a tiny little hamster voice mutter, "Kill Stephan."

This was one of the most popular strips of the year. I remember my wife read it and didn't laugh because she thought it was kind of gross. I thought it was funny, so I ran it. This proves that I am always right and Staci is always wrong.

This has nothing to do with this strip, but I just wanted to say that I will pay dearly for the comment I made below the last one.

In answer to some of the strange e-mail I got about this strip, I just want to say that no, I do not know where Goat could find a typewriter this small.

Sometimes I'm not sure if it's Zebra or the crocs that are supposed to be the sympathetic character in the croc/zebra story line. A better cartoonist would have a handle on this sorta thing.

I really liked this little King series, but it didn't get a huge reaction. I ask that you reconsider it and get back to me.

Tuesday is always my unluckiest day of the week.

The reason for the can, bag, apple core, and banana is that they are the only pieces of trash I can draw. Anything more and I would have exceeded my range.

I once had a syndicated cartoonist tell me that it is "hackwork" to draw yourself into the strip. I'm not sure what that means, but after we talked, I made sure to draw a lot more of myself into the strip.

This was, of course, based on the infamous George W. Bush "Mission Accomplished" sign.

Let me just tell you, Linus' head is impossible to draw.

Larry is apparently much stronger than those stick arms would lead you to believe.

Oh man, this strip really created a problem. I just wanted to do a single strip marking Halloween, so I tucked it in the middle of this "stolen zebra meat" series and didn't think twice about it. But when the "zebra meat" series restarted the next day, everyone wanted to know what happened. Did the croc get the zebra? Is Zebra still alive? I didn't realize it would be taken that way.

Unlike most movies I reference, I actually did see *Little Miss Sunshine*. I thought it was great.

I just realized that in the first panel, it looks like Tata has been impaled on the tail of Rat's speech balloon. I should have drawn it over her, not under her.

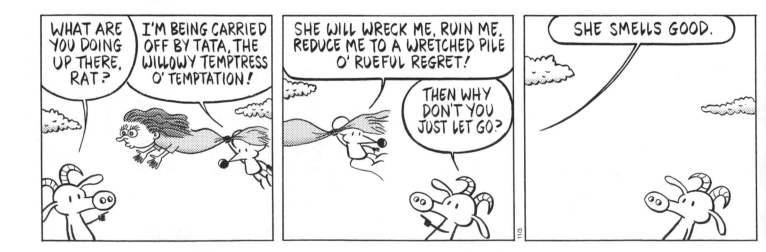

This one is straight out of my own life. Whenever I am on a plane, I will keep the earbuds of my iPod in my ears, whether or not I am listening to music. That way, when the person next to me says something to me, I can pretend I don't hear it. How I then hear the flight attendant when she asks me what I want to drink is a bit of a mystery.

Another day, another croc death. Poor little guys.

I liked Larry's facial expressions in this one. Because the crocs have big googly eyes (as opposed to just dots) and a mouth (something the other characters don't have), I can give them a lot more expression than the other characters.

Note to self: Stop drawing cars.

I know you are, but what am I?

The great part about the Pig-letter-writing strips is if I screw up on the lettering, I just cross it out and make it look like it's Pig's mistake.

For a while there, I got really into reading books about the brain. Eventually, like almost all things I read, it made its way into the strip.

Modern neuroscience would cast doubt on the feasibility of brain function while one's head is being used as a beer cooler.

When I saw the word "hippocampus" in the brain books I read, I knew I had to use it in a strip. It sounds like a place hippopotami would go for higher learning. Whoa—hang on—I just thought of a Pig strip.

I hate those little "My name is" stickers, and when I go to functions where I have to wear one, I almost always take it off. The stupid little thing just screams, "Hey, talk to me. Let's be friends." That's the wrong kind of message to send.

The "Justin" contestant is named after a guy I work with at Creative Associates, Charles Schulz's old studio. Penny is my sister. The brain is a creature of my imagination.

I drew the uncle in the sixth panel to sorta look like one of my wife's real-life uncles, Mike. And I originally called him "Uncle Mike," instead of "Uncle Bob." But I didn't know what he'd think of the strip, so I nixed it. That whole experience with the couple-having-marriage-problems strip made me a little wary.

I didn't really like this week of strips, so I ran them Thanksgiving week, another good time to bury strips you're not sure of.

If I remember right, these "Keel-A-Zeeba-Day" strips were meant to be part of a five-day series, but I didn't like the rest I had written, so I just drew the first two.

Oh man, the week of badness continues. But who knows? Maybe you like them. Don't let me discourage you.

No, no. I was right. They're bad.

My recommendation is to just pull these couple pages out of the book and use them as kindling.

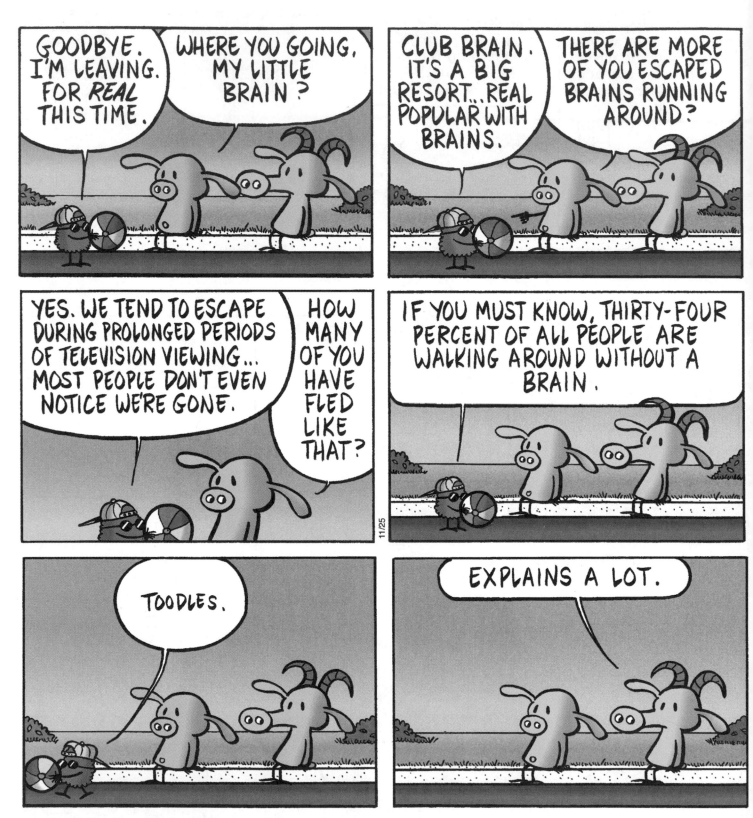

Some readers thought the 34 percent figure was based on George W. Bush's approval rating at the time this strip appeared.

Every now and then, I check out homes for sale in Victoria and Vancouver. They seem like such beautiful places to live.

Whenever Andy appears, I get complaints from animal-rights people saying it is wrong to depict a dog chained to a stake. And some of the e-mails are amazingly hate filled. But for me, Andy is just a metaphor meant to symbolize how we learn to live within the limitations imposed on us. And Andy thrives under those conditions. He is the most optimistic character in the strip. So hey—all you complainers—you're kinda dumb.

Whenever Rat does a strip about Goat's blog, the strip gets posted on tons of people's real-life blogs. Blog writers on the whole seem to be a good bunch of sports. I should introduce them to the un-good bunch of sports that write to me about Andy.

215

Every now and then, I like to show that Rat has one or two good qualities. Well, two might be pushing it.

See, Andy is hopeful. He is not a bitter, sad-faced whiner. Which is more than I can say about the people who complain about him. Ohhhhh, snap!

I believe this is the one and only time I have ever drawn snow in the strip. As someone who has lived his entire life in California (and rarely visits the Sierras), snow is just not part of my life.

Some people—people with inappropriate, filth-covered brains—had a much different interpretation of the first panel. Shame. Shame. Shame.

This strip is one of the few times Rat shows some self-knowledge, i.e., that he is not a good guy. I don't do it very often with him, because his exaggerated sense of self is really the key to his character.

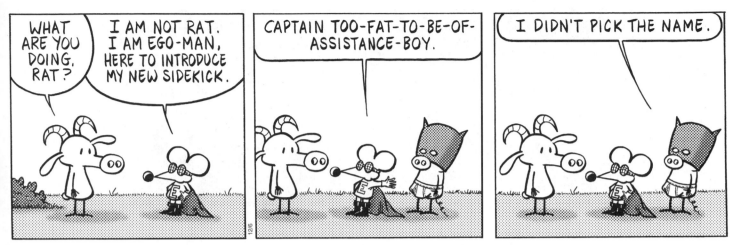

Because so many people wanted to see Ego-Man again, I brought him back.

For the record, I wear boxers, not briefs. You probably didn't want to know that.

Every Christmas season, I drive my kids around the neighborhood and we rank the neighbors' Christmas decorations from a scale of 0 (bad) to 10 (good). Unlike Guard Duck, we *like* the deer and actually give a point for each illuminated deer the person has. If the deer's head also moves, we give *two* points.

More brain strips from my brain-book-reading days. I really liked this one.

A rare strip where I don't draw any floor line in that last panel, so the wall just kind of blends in with the floor. Ohhh, the artistic variety that is *Pearls*.

The stuff they're stringing there is popcorn, in case you were saying to yourself, "Hey, what's that crap on the floor?" Oh, and that's a fire in the fireplace.

Having the croc dress as a murderous Joseph triggered some complaints . . .

. . . but not as many complaints as making him Jesus.

And "bite me" is a phrase that is almost guaranteed to anger some older readers. Apparently, this was "Which Strip Can Tick Off the Most Readers?" week in *Pearls*.

I must admit, I've never owned or even once used a BlackBerry. I don't see the appeal of always being in contact with other people.

I'm getting better at drawing couches. At least you know they're couches. Which is more than I can say about the fire I drew on December 11, 2007.

Around this time, people started to complain about how dark this story line was.

But see, it had a happy ending! Okay, not totally happy. The guy had one of his legs chewed off, but still, for *Pearls*, that's pretty happy.

I never, ever recline my seat on an airplane if there is someone sitting behind me. Maybe it's because I'm over six feet tall, but when someone does it to me, it makes the flight very uncomfortable. So if you are sitting on an airplane right now reading this book and there is a guy with a goatee and a backward cap behind you, please return your seat to the upright position.

My little tribute to my cartooning hero, Charles Schulz.

This is a rare one, in that the joke was suggested to me by my editor at United. I rarely—in fact, almost never—take ideas from other people.

Dogs that are high on drugs can cause problems with touchy readers. So I buried this strip in the days after Christmas.

This one was so strange and un-good that I almost didn't run it. There was also a second strip in this series that was even worse, so I killed that one. The killed strip is printed for the first time in the "Stuff You Ain't Never Seen Before" section of this book.

Okay, this was a good strip. I'm not sure why I tucked it into the days after Christmas.

My wife and I fight every time we go on vacation. She probably doesn't want me telling you that, so I'm gonna keep this book away from her. If you meet her, don't say anything.

I like shoving Rat's head into things.

I really liked these three lion strips. I thought this was the best of the three.

230

Why do Nigerians keep sending these e-mails? Is anyone in the world fooled? Well, other than Pig?

Rat's line in the second panel is a paraphrase of a Simon and Garfunkel lyric ("Still the man hears what he wants to hear and disregards the rest").

The part about this strip that I liked was the croc's line in the first panel: "Dis is all-powerful, all-loving Box God . . . He hate you."

I take the world's longest showers. It's the best twenty-five minutes of the day.

This was a great strip in my little head. Until I had to keep drawing all those remora. Then I thought the idea was terrible.

This was a reference to the famous Groucho Marx game show, *You Bet Your Life.* When the contestant said the secret word, this duck dropped down from the sky and the contestant won money. Given that I had never actually used the phrase "pearls before swine" in the strip, I thought it would work well here.

Look how much fatter the remora are here than they were in the first strip. I guess they've been eating barnacles off Pig.

I think other people are so great when I'm drunk. That's why they call it "impaired judgment."

This strip generated a huge response. People seemed to really like it. The creator of the real *Slylock Fox* strip, Bob Weber Jr., was a great sport about it. In fact, a few weeks later, he incorporated Rat into his own strip, using him as the main suspect in a crime. The only complaints this triggered were for the reference to Hitler. There are a number of people out there who believe strongly that you should never use his name in any joke, as it purportedly makes light of what he did. I don't agree, but that doesn't stop them from writing angry e-mail.

I think the original British version of *The Office* is the greatest television comedy ever made. I like the American version also, but not as much as the British one.

The roof fish were very popular characters. See, I'm making up for that really bad week in late November.

Rat's thoughts in the first panel are mine as well. I can almost never enjoy success. I view it almost as a jinx on my future prospects.

For those of you who don't know this little game, the person says, "Pull my finger," and when you do, they fart. The great part about putting it in the strip is that the type of people who would be most offended have no idea what the game is, so they don't complain. Stephan: 1. Complainers: 0.

Probably one of the most popular croc strips I have ever done. So much so that I made it the cover of the 2010 *Pearls* wall calendar, the title of which is *And Da Wind Cry Moron.*

Suits are hard for me to draw. But these came out okay. Now if I can just learn how to draw cars.

Wow, look at the shape of the man's head change from the second to the third panel. He must be like Gumby or something.

This is a really old strip that I held on to for a while. You can tell by how small the lettering is compared to the other strips.

240

Proof that the croc can actually cross over the hedge that separates his yard from Zebra's (although it might take a shove from his wife).

I never get complaints from short people when I do strips like this. From this I conclude that all short people have a great sense of humor.

I liked this strip. I hereby use it to cancel out one of those bad ones from that miserable week in November.

Another really old strip that I delayed running, probably because I didn't like it that much. Again, you can tell from the small size of the dialogue.

Confession time: I am forty years old and popping bubble wrap can entertain me for a full hour.

I believe I wrote at least five of these strips, but only drew the first one. Whenever you do Osama bin Laden jokes, you always get complainers, and I didn't want to get complaints for a full week. Plus, I wasn't convinced as to its funniness. I think I regret that now. This might have been a decent series.

Rat always drinks beer when writing "Angry Bob." I think this was the first time he's had martinis instead.

This was a popular strip. I think a lot of people related to it. As I think I've said before, a so-so joke that everyone relates to will go over much bigger than a strong joke that's just sort of bizarre and esoteric.

A lot of people ask me how many crocs have died in the strip. I used to keep track, but lost count after around forty or so.

For those of you who haven't heard of it, Beano is a product you buy that helps control flatulence.

And the reference here is to the U2 song, "Where the Streets Have No Name." The song's opening lyrics are: "I want to run. I want to hide. I want to tear down the walls that hold me inside." It's off an album called *The Joshua Tree,* which may be my all-time favorite album.

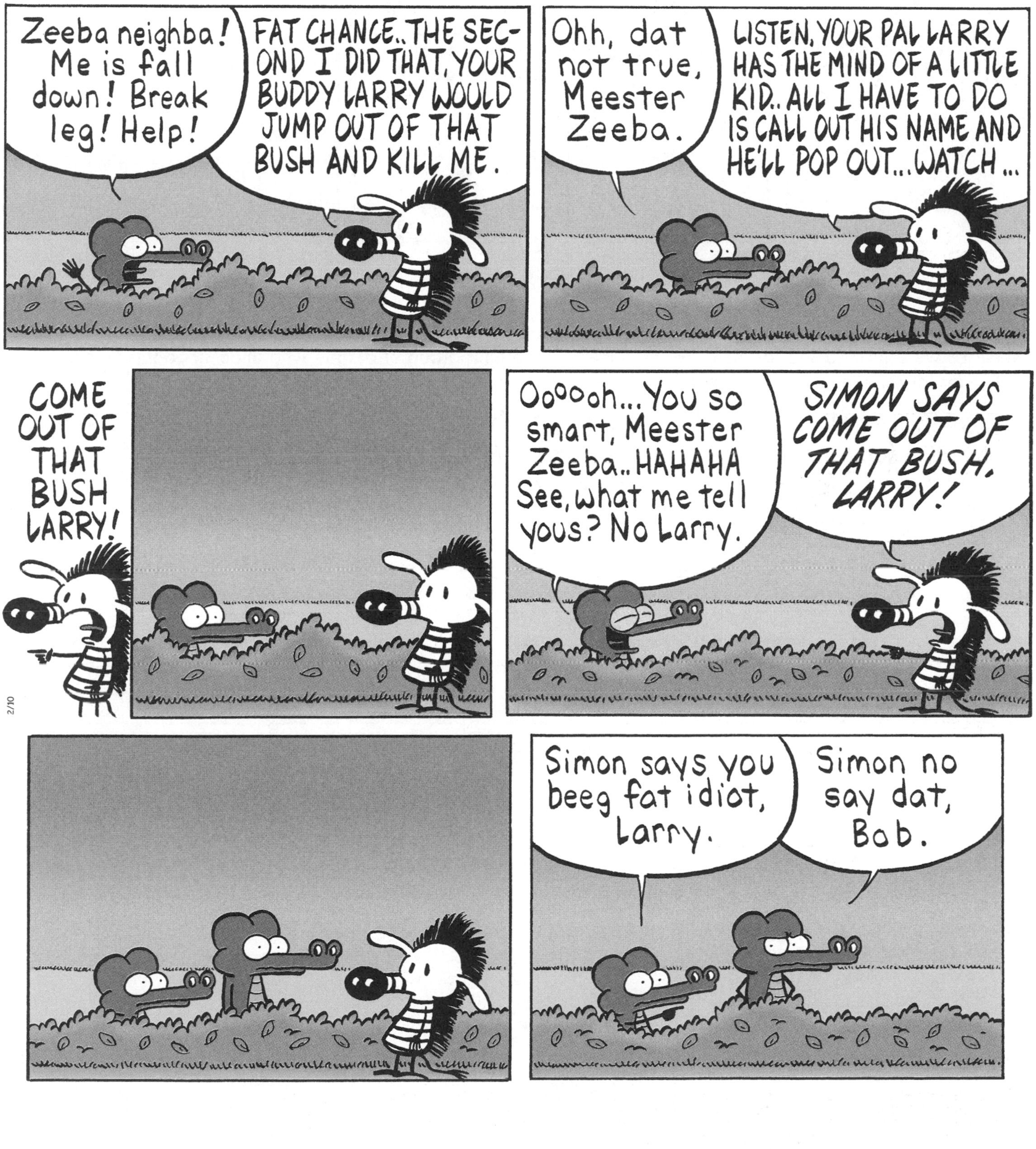

Zeeba neighba! Me is fall down! Break leg! Help!
FAT CHANCE.. THE SECOND I DID THAT, YOUR BUDDY LARRY WOULD JUMP OUT OF THAT BUSH AND KILL ME.
Ohh, dat not true, Meester Zeeba.
LISTEN, YOUR PAL LARRY HAS THE MIND OF A LITTLE KID.. ALL I HAVE TO DO IS CALL OUT HIS NAME AND HE'LL POP OUT... WATCH...
COME OUT OF THAT BUSH LARRY!
Ooooh... You so smart, Meester Zeeba.. HAHAHA See, what me tell yous? No Larry.
SIMON SAYS COME OUT OF THAT BUSH, LARRY!
Simon says you beeg fat idiot, Larry.
Simon no say dat, Bob.
2/10

Boy, was the reaction to these strips split. From the animal-rights activists, there were even more complaints, because now there were *two* chained dogs. Then there was a second group of people who complained because the strips were just too sad for them. But then there was a third group of people who understood this was a metaphor for people who love each other but cannot physically touch each other.

A lot of people wanted reprints of this strip. Except for the animal-rights people. They just wanted the series to end.

A nice, sweet, uplifting strip to run on Valentine's Day.

This was a very popular strip. So popular we put it on a shirt that we sell from the *Pearls* Web site (www.comics.com/pearls_before_swine).

This was based on a real guy at my gym who smelled worse than any human being alive has ever smelled. Perhaps worse than any dead human as well.

Stuff You Ain't Never Seen Before

The following eighteen strips are all strips that were pulled prior to publication, either because they posed too much of a risk, were too strange, or were just plain bad. I leave you to be the judge. But please, have mercy.

I didn't think this one was superfunny, and the subject matter can pose some difficulties among more conservative papers. Given that the funniness potential didn't justify even the small risk, I pulled it.

This is the original "mescaline" version of the October 14, 2006, strip.

Between the reference to blind people and the reference to "copping a feel," this just had "letters to the editor" written all over it. More important, it wasn't that funny, so I nixed it.

This was the other bird strip that was supposed to go along with the December 9, 2006, bird strip. But I just thought it was kind of weak, so I pulled it.

After the experience with the croc-getting-strangled strip (July 5, 2007), I became a little more hesitant about actually showing the crocs dying. Also, the image of the croc dangling there in the last panel seemed a bit dark.

I just didn't think this one was very good, so I kept delaying its publication. Finally, I pulled it altogether.

Ditto on this one. I just didn't like the joke. And if a talking-head strip has weak writing, it really doesn't have anything else to offer.

This was the strip that was supposed to follow the December 28, 2007, strip, but it was just too strange (even for me), so I nixed it.

This is one of the alternate punch line versions of the January 23, 2007, strip. Looking back on it, it's probably better than the one I ran.

STORY REFRESHER: Rat, in the midst of his representing the crocs in their lawsuit against Zebra, found out that his girlfriend, Farina, was cheating on him in Florida. Traveling to Florida in his astronaut helmet and diapers, Rat and his Revenge-O' Mobile broke down in Arizona, where Rat was captured by a gang of angry "Family Circus" fans.

This strip was supposed to run in the midst of the *Family Circus*/astronaut story line in September 2007. It was making fun of a story arc in the comic strip *Funky Winkerbean* where a character named Lisa had a fatal disease and then did not have a fatal disease and then had it again, or something like that. I showed it to Tom Batiuk, the creator of *Funky Winkerbean*, and he could not have been a better sport about it. But the whole *Funky Winkerbean* "Lisa" story line became a huge national story where readers debated whether or not a topic as serious as cancer should be fodder for the comics page, and I didn't want to be in the middle of that. Plus, even though I didn't mention cancer, many comics readers familiar with *Funky Winkerbean* would know the disease being referenced here was, in fact, cancer, and the you-know-what would have hit the fan. So after a long debate with myself, I pulled it.

Religious references always bring out the biggest whack-job complainers. Between that and the fact that this joke was kind of weak, I decided not to run the strip.

Man, I must have gone back and forth on running this about a million times. What finally made me not run it was that the joke only works if you know the swear word, and I didn't want nine million kids asking their parents what the word was, and the parents writing to me and their newspaper editor.

This is one I tried to run, but my syndicate asked me not to. It's ironic that a strip that's about the censorship of the word "sucks" ended up being censored. That sucks.

This strip was supposed to run in the "National Enquirat" series, but I was worried about all the complaints I would get from both Christians and Jews. Looking back on it, I think it was a pretty funny strip. I should have run it.

This strip was just plain bad. With great shame, I present it to you now.

The word that "horticulture" plays off of here is a word you couldn't use on the comics page. Also, at the time I drew it, Jerry Falwell was alive. But then he died. So between the concern over the "horticulture" pun and the mockery of a dead guy, this was just too risky. I did, however, think it was a decent strip.

I showed this to both my wife and to Darby Conley (*Get Fuzzy*) and they both thought it was dumb, so I pulled it. I rarely do that with a Sunday strip, but looking back on it, I can see they were right.

This strip was making fun of the conservative writer Bill Bennett. But at this point in the development of *Pearls*, I really wasn't interested in doing these kind of "political" strips. At least not overtly so. I mean, there are ways to comment on these issues in the subtext of the strip without having to be so blatant. Thus, I nixed it.

And on that apolitical note, I say good-bye until the next treasury.